Editor
Sarah Beatty

Managing Editor
Ina Massler Levin, M.A.

Editor-in-Chief
Sharon Coan, M.S. Ed.

Illustrator
Blanca Apodaca

Cover Artist
Denise Bauer

Art Coordinator
Kevin Barnes

Imaging
James Edward Grace
Rosa C. See
Alfred Lau

Product Manager
Phil Garcia

Publishers
Rachelle Cracchiolo, M.S. Ed.
Mary Dupuy Smith, M.S. Ed.

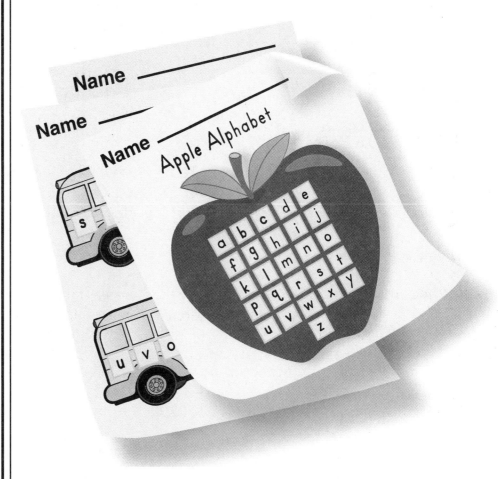

Authors

Kathy Crane and Kathleen Law

Teacher Created Materials, Inc.
6421 Industry Way
Westminster, CA 92683
www.teachercreated.com
ISBN-0-7439-3266-8
©2002 Teacher Created Materials, Inc.
Made in U.S.A.

Table of Contents

Table of Contents *(cont.)*

Introduction

Through songs, rhymes, and books, phonological awareness has always been a part of the kindergarten experience. Recent research has indicated, however, that more time needs to be spent in this discipline. Furthermore, phonological awareness must move along a continuum from syllables and rhymes to phonemic awareness, an awareness of individual phonemes within words.

Research has also determined that two of the greatest factors in determining the success of a young reader are phonemic awareness and alphabet recognition. This collection of phonological awareness and alphabet lessons was written in response to this research.

The lessons have been placed in an order that reflects a research-based phonological scope and sequence. Although your class may not need to complete every lesson, it is best to complete them in order rather than skipping around. Many of the lessons build on one another. For example, counting individual words helps students listen for syllables, syllable identification helps students recognize individual phonemes, and listening for individual phonemes helps prepare students for segmentation.

Phonological awareness activities should be completed orally. In a regular kindergarten classroom, students should be engaged in phonological awareness for at least 15 minutes each day. An additional 15 minutes should be spent in alphabet recognition; this time is more meaningful when students have a variety of alphabet experiences as well as opportunities to work with letter manipulatives. After developing a firm foundation in both phonological awareness and in alphabet recognition, phonics skills, those connecting sounds to letters, can be introduced.

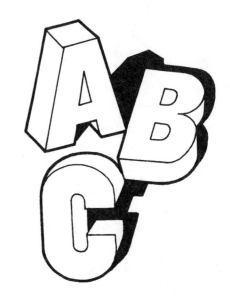

As students develop phonological awareness, alphabet recognition, and phonics skills, it is important to provide an environment that encourages risk-taking. Keep the atmosphere light and supportive. If student attention wanders, change the lesson or take a break. Assist students when necessary, but plan to provide additional practice at another time.

Although this book addresses all areas of the language arts curriculum—speaking, listening, reading, and writing—the lessons focus primarily on two areas of reading instruction that are crucial to the development of beginning readers. With the activities in this book, you can address this critical need through games, hands-on activities, movement, and a spirit of fun.

Materials

Many of the lessons in this book use basic materials found in most kindergarten classrooms. Additional materials can be made using the work sheets provided in the book. The following items (or substitute items) will be needed. They will add variety to the activities while engaging additional senses.

- magnetic and/or tactile letters
- magnet board
- easel
- pocket chart
- small objects
- small baskets or tubs
- picture cards
- lowercase and capital letter cards of varying sizes
- generic game board

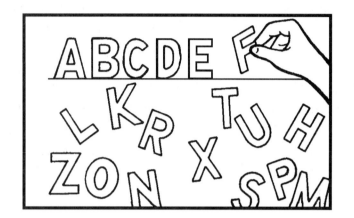

The small objects will be used for rhyming and segmenting lessons as well as for initial sound activities. While any small object can be used, you will need multiple items beginning with the same sound. Small tubs of objects can be purchased or you can collect your own objects, using the ones that fit the lesson best. If necessary, substitute picture cards for objects.

Flashcards or letter cards are also used in multiple lessons. A set of capital letters and a set of lowercase letters are included in this book. To make them more durable, copy onto tagboard and laminate before using them. The capital and the lowercase letters need to be different colors for one of the lessons.

Picture cards are frequently used. You can purchase picture cards or make your own using the various picture-card work sheets provided in the book. The cards provided in this book include the name of the picture in small print. This is for teacher use and can be removed with a correction pen if the words would distract the students. As with all of the material in the book, if you color and laminate the picture cards before cutting them apart, they will be more attractive and durable. When deciding how to prepare the materials, consider your time, expense, and expected frequency of use of the material.

Game boards are needed for a number of lessons. You can substitute one large commercial or homemade game board for any game. Game board masters are included in the book; however, it is best to give each student an individual game board when using them because of their size. Games are played the same whether you use one large board or multiple small boards.

How To Use This Book

All of the following developmentally appropriate lessons were designed for use with a small group of kindergartners. The size of your group will need to be determined by a number of factors, however. The amount of material available, the size of your class, the number of helpers assisting you, and the academic needs of your students must be taken into account. Many of the lessons can be introduced to a large group and repeated in small groups if students need additional help. Most lessons can be completed with one student if you need to individualize instruction.

Many of the activities in this book are "old favorites" that can be found in other sources. The ideas have been incorporated into a lesson that can be used by a parent volunteer or a classroom aide.

Each lesson follows the same format.

- The title indicates which skill will be reviewed.
- The objective states the goal of the lesson.
- The rationale explains why this objective is important.
- The materials section lists the items needed for the lesson.
- The preparation section explains how to prepare the materials and/or where to find them. Usually the necessary work sheets will be found immediately following the lesson, unless the same materials have been used for another lesson.

The lesson begins after the preparation section.
- Each lesson is scripted.
- The teacher or assistant reads the bold portion aloud to the students.
- The regular print indicates what the teacher or assistant should do to complete the lesson. This portion of the lesson should not be read aloud since it is only for the information of the teacher.

These lessons are followed by an index. The index lists the activities according to reading standards for kindergarten.

On another note, references are made to letters and to sounds throughout the book. *Sounds are indicated with a slash before and after the letter. For example, /s/ should be said sssssssssssssssss, not s. Phonemic awareness deals with sounds, not letter names.*

Familiar Sounds

Objective: Listening to familiar sounds

Rationale: Listening is a necessary skill for developing readers.

Materials: A tape recording of everyday sounds

Preparation: To prepare this tape, choose sounds that are easy to identify and easy for you to record. Include sounds such as a telephone ringing, a radio playing, a horn honking, a school bell ringing, a door slamming, a dog barking, a cat meowing, hands clapping, fingers snapping, water running, a toilet flushing, a piano playing, and/or a doorbell ringing. People engaged in various activities can also be recorded—children playing, a woman talking, a man singing, children laughing, a baby crying, a man whistling, and/or a woman humming. Record at least 15 sounds; each sound should last for two to five seconds. Leave approximately 10 seconds of space between sounds so you can easily turn the recording on and off between sounds.

Procedure:

- Seat the children in a semicircle on the floor.
- **Today we are going to play a listening game.**
- **I am going to play several sounds that will probably be familiar to you.**
- **Listen carefully, then name the sound on the tape.**
- Play the tape. Push pause after each sound to allow for student response.

Variation 1: Play the tape; push pause after two sounds. Have students identify the first and the last sounds. To challenge students, play three sounds. Have students name the first, middle, and last sounds.

Variation 2: Make a sound around the room (shut the door, sharpen a pencil, etc.) while students sit with eyes closed. Have students explain how the sound was made.

How Many Words?

Objective: Recognizing words in speech

Rationale: Identifying separate words lays the foundation for identifying syllables and phonemes.

Materials: None

Preparation: None

Procedure:

- Seat the children around you.
- **Listen to this sentence: Mary had a Little Lamb.**
- **This sentence is made of words. As I say it again, I'm going to put up a finger for each word.**
- Repeat the sentence, putting up one finger for each word.
- **Now let's see how many fingers I have raised.** (Count your fingers.)
- **There are five words in the sentence, Mary had a Little Lamb.**
- **Now, I am going to have one child come up and stand in a line for each word. Our sentence has five words, so I will need five children.**
- Call up five children and have them stand in a line. Walk behind the children, placing your hand above the head of one child for each word as you say the sentence.
- **Okay, let's try another sentence from a nursery rhyme.**
- Repeat the process using one line at a time from several nursery rhymes.
- Continue as long as time permits.

What Do You Hear?

Objective: Identifying sounds

Rationale: Identifying the sounds around us lays the foundation for identifying the separate sounds within words.

Materials: None

Preparation: None

Procedure:

- Shut the classroom door before beginning this lesson.

- **Close your eyes and listen.** (Pause for five to ten seconds.)

- **What do you hear? Close your eyes and listen again. Do you hear any other sounds?**

- **We can learn a lot if we listen carefully to sounds. Today we are going to take a walk around our school. We will name the sounds that we hear. Line up quietly behind me, and we will begin.**

- Lead the students into the hall.

- **Close your eyes and listen.** (Pause.) **What do you hear?**

- Walk to another area in your school. Have the students pause and listen before naming sounds in that area.

- Continue the activity around your school. Try to pick areas where you will hear different sounds – the gym, the office area, the computer lab, the library, etc.

- **Now let's go outside. Close your eyes and listen. What sounds do you hear?**

- Choose another outside location if the sounds will be different in that area.

- Return to the room within the allotted time.

Counting Words

Objective: Recognizing words in speech

Rationale: Identifying separate words lays the foundation for identifying syllables.

Materials: A work mat for each student (a piece of construction paper can be used as a work mat), Bingo markers or some kind of counter

Preparation: None

Procedure:

- Seat the children around you. **Listen to this sentence:** *I like to play.* **This sentence is made of words. As I say it again, I'm going to put a counter down for each word.** Repeat the sentence, laying a counter down as you say each word. **Now let's see how many counters I have on the mat.** (Count the 4 markers.) **There are four words in the sentence,** *I like to play.*

- **Let's count words in sentences that we make up. Who has something to tell us?** Pause. Call on a volunteer or prompt a student if no one says anything. When a sentence is given, repeat it, rephrasing if necessary. Wordy sentences (*I went to McDonald's with my mom and baby brother and I played and I got a toy.*) can be shortened (*I went to McDonald's.*).

- Give each student a work mat and some counters. Have each student place the counters beside the mat. **Let's put a counter on the mat for every word that we say. The sentence is** (repeat student's sentence). **Now let's say it together one word at a time.**

- Say the first word of the sentence with the students and place a counter on your mat. Check that each student has successfully placed a counter on his/her mat. Say the second word with the students, placing a second counter on your mat. Continue until the sentence is complete.

- **How many counters are on your mat? Let's count together. We have _____ counters, so the sentence has _____ words. Let's count on our fingers as we say the sentence again.**

- Repeat the sentence slowly, holding up one finger for every word. Keep holding up your fingers. **The sentence has _____ words. Who else has something to tell us?** Repeat the procedure. Continue as long as time permits.

Alphabet Song

Objective: Building an awareness of the alphabet

Rationale: Singing the alphabet song and listening to alphabet books will help students become familiar with letter names.

Materials: A pointer, alphabet chart

Preparation: None

Procedure:

- Seat the children so they can see the alphabet on the wall or on a chart.
- **Sing the alphabet song with me. A, B, C, D....**
- Continue singing the entire song. Point to each letter as you sing the song.
- **Let's sing the song again. Who would like to point to the letters with me?**
- Hand the pointer to a student. Assist if necessary so the child points to the correct letter.
- Repeat the song, allowing a different student to point to the letters.
- Return to this activity frequently so all students eventually have the opportunity to point to the letters.

Note: Include at least one alphabet activity in your daily plans. Sing the alphabet song and point to letters, read an alphabet book, review alphabet flashcards, and/or plan hands-on alphabet activities for small group practice during learning centers.

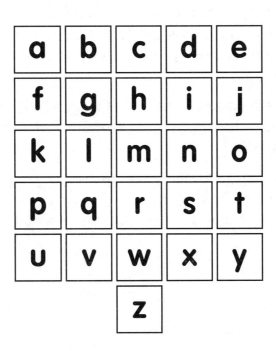

Alphabet Bear Match

Objective: Matching uppercase letters of the alphabet

Rationale: Initial letter recognition activities should focus on capital letters since they are more difficult to confuse than lowercase letters.

Materials: Alphabet Bear Match game cards (page 13), bears with capital letters (pages 12, 14–16), basket (optional)

Preparation: Copy six game cards. Write a different capital letter in each space. (If you make six game cards, you will be able to write in 24 different letters; skip the letters X and Z since there are no corresponding bears for those letters.) Cut out one copy of each bear and place it in a basket. (If you want a durable set of materials to use again and again, copy the game cards and the bears onto tag and laminate them before using. You may choose to color selected portions or copy them onto colored tag.)

Procedure:

- Seat the children around a table. Give each child an Alphabet Bear Match game card. Students should be able to reach a basket filled with letter bears.

- **We're going to play Alphabet Bear Match. Each of you will have a turn drawing a bear out of a basket. If it matches a letter on your card, you will place it on your card. If not, place it back in the basket.**

- **Okay, (student's name) you go first. Choose a bear.**

- **What letter is on your bear? Do you have that letter on your game card? If you do, put the bear on top of his match. If not, put him back in the basket.**

- Continue play around the table until all players have covered their cards. Trade cards and begin again.

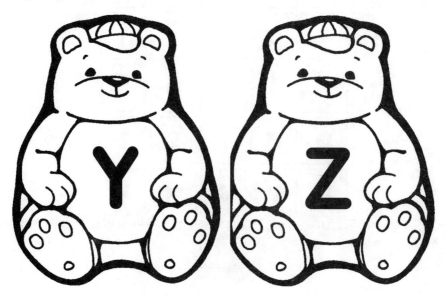

Alphabet Bear Match Game Card

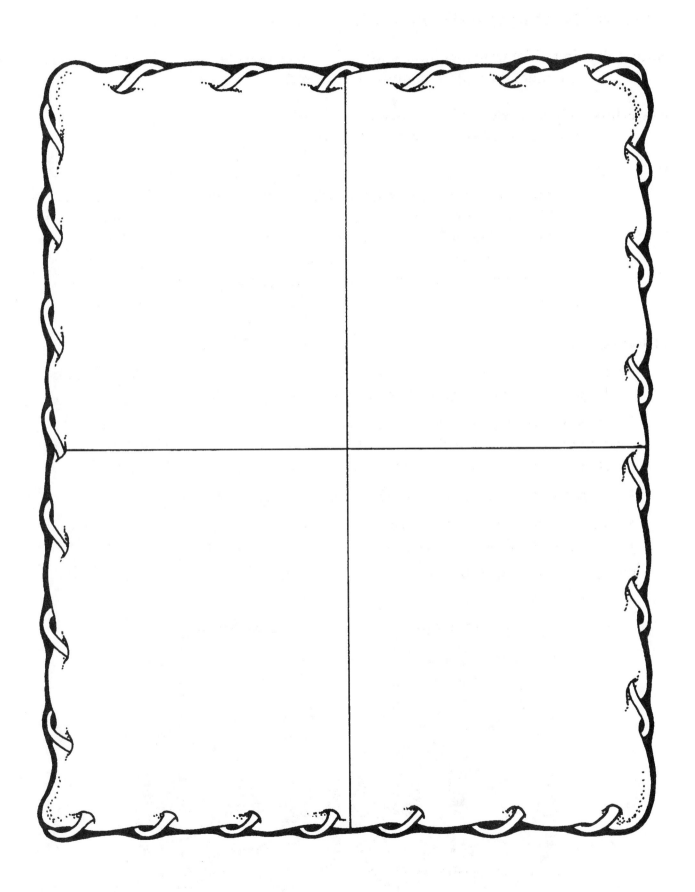

Alphabet Bears

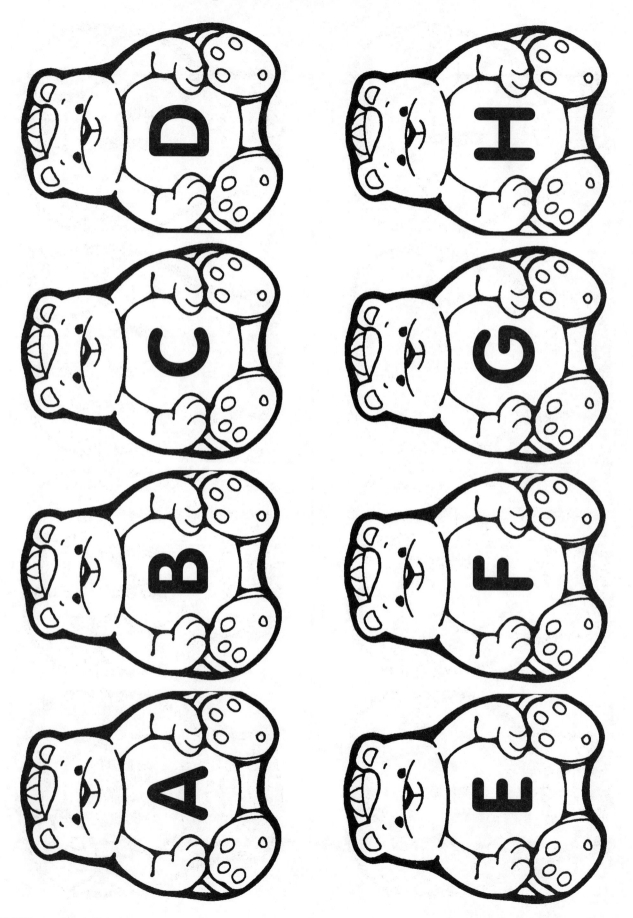

14

Alphabet Bears *(cont.)*

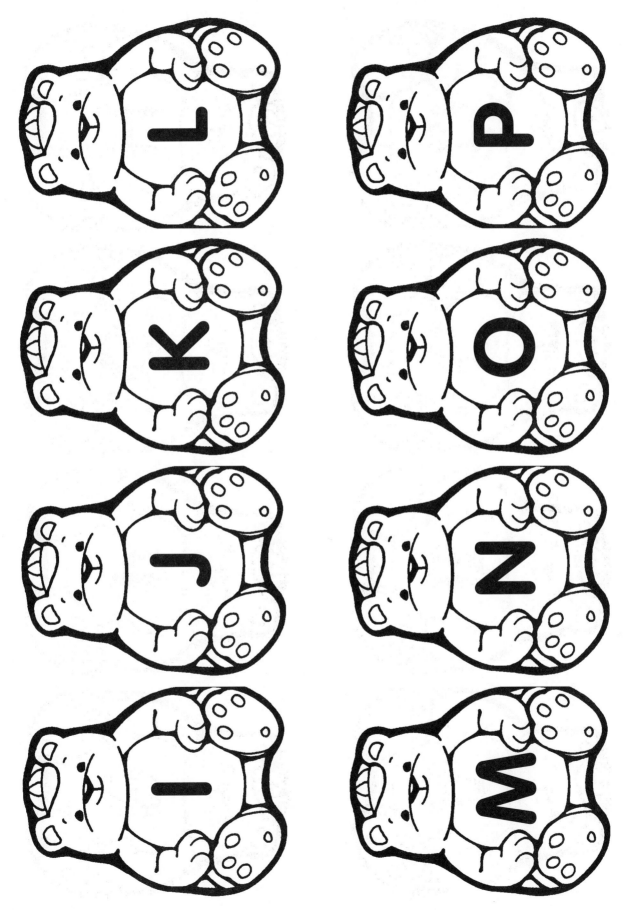

Alphabet Bears *(cont.)*

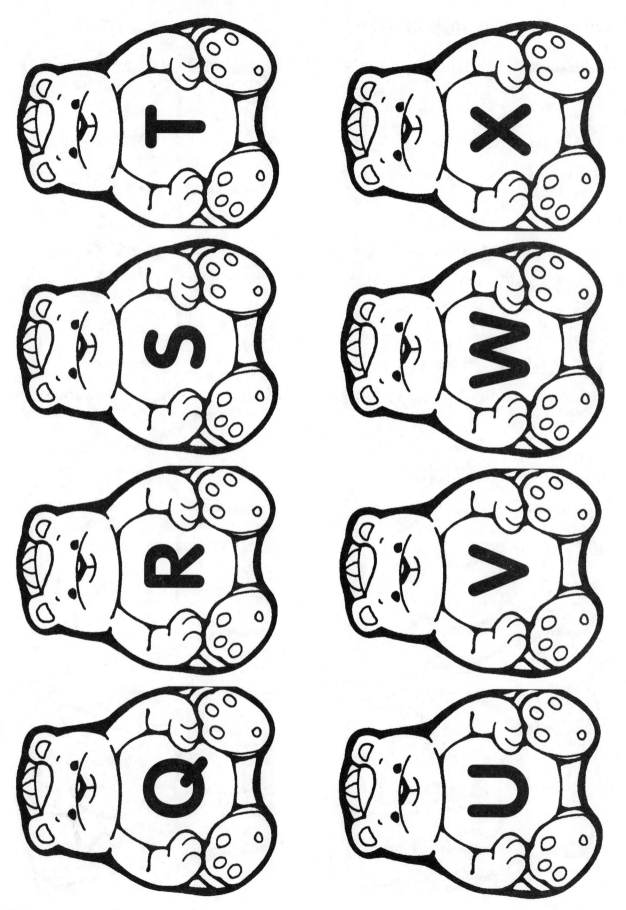

Rhymes in Books

Objective: Identifying rhyming words

Rationale: Literature with a rhyming text captures students' interest while building their phonological awareness skills. Youngsters love to have delightful stories read to them again and again.

Materials: Any rhyming book

Preparation: None

Procedure:

- Seat the children in a semicircle on the floor.
- Tell the children that you are going to read (*name of book*).
- Have the children look at the cover.
- **What do you think this story will be about?**
- Accept the students' predictions.
- **This book is full of rhyming words. Please listen for them as I read the story.**
- Read the story to the children.
- **I am going to read this story again. This time when I pause, please help me supply the missing word.**
- Reread the story, pausing before the rhyming word. Allow the children to supply it. As they say the word, quickly nod and echo the correct answer. If they cannot supply it, simply tell them the word and continue reading.

Rhyming Characters

Objective: Identifying rhyming words

Rationale: Children build confidence in rhyming as they participate in activities using favorite books.

Materials: A rhyming book with animal characters such as *Silly Sally* (Wood, Audrey. Harcourt Brace & Company, 1992.), chart paper, marker, plain white paper, crayons

Preparation: None

Procedure:

- Seat the children in a semicircle on the floor. Show the children the cover of the book you have selected. **What do you think this story will be about?** Accept the students' predictions.

- **This book is full of rhyming words. Please listen for them as I read the story.** Read the story to the children. Discuss some of the rhymes.

- **Let's think of some more rhymes for one of the animal characters. In the book *Silly Sally*, a pig danced a jig. (Student's name), what else rhymes with pig?**

- **Now let's think of some rhymes for other animals that could be characters in a book.**

- Make a list of animals. As a student makes up a rhyme for an animal, write the word in the next column.

Example	
duck	truck
cat	hat
dog	log
mouse	house

- Give each child a piece of paper. **Let's each draw a picture of a new animal character.**

- Have each student draw one of the new animal characters. Write the rhyme, such as, *a duck driving a truck.* At the end of the lesson, you may wish to bind the pages together to make a class book.

Rhyming Objects

Objective: Identifying rhyming objects

Rationale: This is a hands–on review of rhyming words.

Materials: A box of rhyming objects

Preparation: Use a commercial set of rhyming objects or gather items from around the classroom that form rhyming sets. Picture cards can be substituted for objects if necessary. (Possible objects include: shell/bell, car/star, block/sock, fan/can, snake/cake, mug/rug, dog/log, bone/cone, and ring/king.)

Procedure:

- Seat the children at a table.

- Show the students the objects in the box one by one. Name the objects with the students as you lay them out on the table. Then, return objects to the box.

- Ask a student volunteer to take two objects from the box.

- **What are the names of your objects?**

- **Let's see if these objects rhyme. _____ and _____. Do they rhyme?**

- As the students respond, congratulate them on their ability to identify objects that are rhyming or non-rhyming pairs.

- If a student chooses items that do not rhyme, identify them as a non-rhyming pair and continue around the table. When the same student has another turn, however, encourage him/her to choose a rhyming pair in order to review and reinforce rhymes. Help the student match rhyming objects if necessary.

- Continue the activity around the table, allowing each child to have several turns retrieving two objects from the box.

Find the Rhyme

Objective: Identifying rhyming words

Rationale: This is a hands-on review of rhyming words.

Materials: Rhyming picture cards (pages 21–23)

Preparation: Color and laminate (optional) the rhyming picture cards. Cut the rhyming cards apart and put into sets of three, with two rhyming pictures and one non-rhyming picture. Arrange each set so a rhyming picture is first; vary the order of the other two cards within each set.

Procedure:

- Seat the children around a table.
- **Today we are going to play a rhyming game called Find the Rhyme.**
- Lay the first set of picture cards in a row on the table.
- **(Student's name), would you like to go first? Let's name the pictures together. _____, _____, and _____. Which one rhymes with _____** (Name the first card.)**?**
- **You're right! _____ rhymes with _____. Let's try that again with a different set of pictures.**
- Lay three more pictures down.
- Turn to the next student. **Let's name the pictures together. _____, _____, and _____. Which one rhymes with _____?**
- Continue the activity around the group.

Rhyming Picture Cards

pan

can

boat

goat

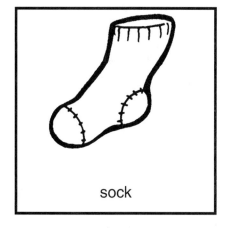

sock

rock

sun

bun

rose

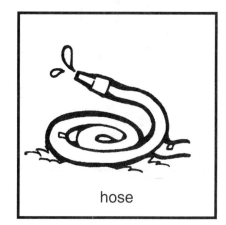

hose

Rhyming Picture Cards *(cont.)*

mouse

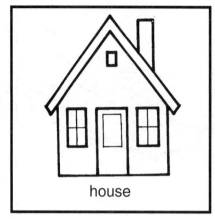

house

bee

tree

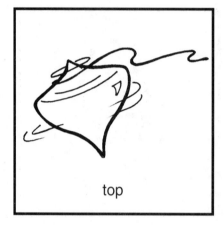

top

mop

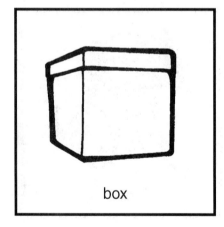

box

fox

clock

lock

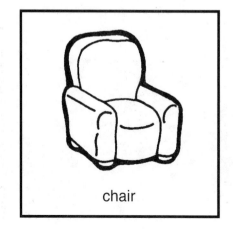

chair

bear

Rhyming Picture Cards *(cont.)*

cat

hat

ice

mice

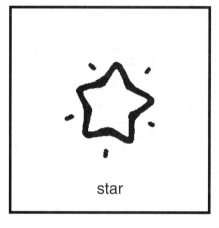

star

car

king

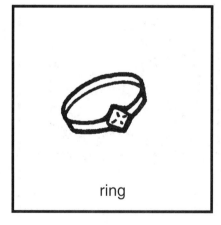

ring

dog

log

bug

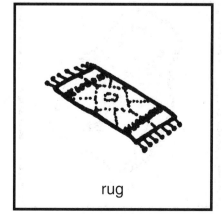

rug

Alphabet Bingo

Objective: Recognizing letters of the alphabet

Rationale: Reviewing the alphabet through a game will enhance letter recognition.

Materials: An Alphabet Bingo card for each player (page 25), letter cards (pages 26–31), Bingo markers

Preparation: Copy a Bingo card for each player, then write a letter in each space. Vary the letters on each card. Laminate the Bingo cards and the letter cards if desired. Cut the letter cards apart.

Procedure:

- Seat the children around a table. Give each child a Bingo card. Students should be able to reach a basket or pile of Bingo markers.

- **We're going to play Alphabet Bingo today. You will put a Bingo marker on each letter as I say its name. When I have called all of the letters on your card, say *Bingo*. Let's begin.**

- Draw a card and say the letter. Pause. Repeat the letter and show the letter card. Check student cards to make sure everyone understands how to play the game.

- Draw another card and repeat the process. Keep playing until you have called all the letters. Allow each student to call out Bingo when he/she covers all the letters on his/her card.

- Trade cards and play the game again if time permits.

Variation 1: Show an alphabet card to the students; ask them to name the letter. Repeat the letter name and make the letter sound for the students.

Variation 2: Make the sound of a letter. Ask the students to name the letter. Repeat (or tell) the letter's name and show the card to the students.

Note: It is best to introduce Alphabet Bingo in a small group setting so you can monitor student progress. After that the game can be played with large or small groups.

Alphabet Bingo

Alphabet Cards

A	B	C
D	E	F
G	H	I

Alphabet Cards *(cont.)*

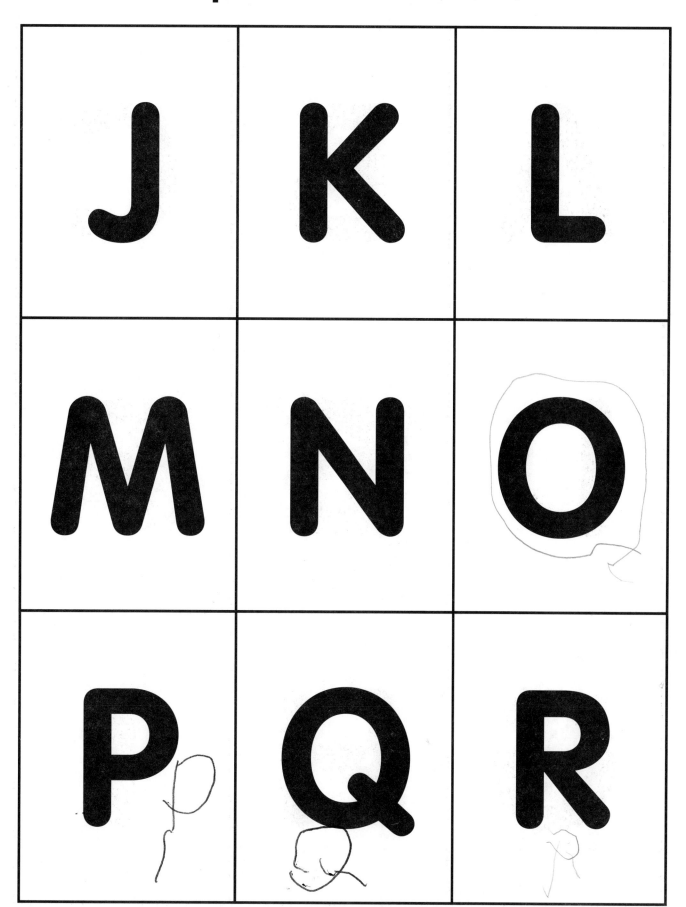

J	K	L
M	N	O
P	Q	R

Alphabet Cards *(cont.)*

S	T	U
V	W	X
Y	Z	

Alphabet Cards *(cont.)*

a	b	c
d	e	f
g	h	i

Alphabet Cards *(cont.)*

j	k	l
m	n	o
p	q	r

Alphabet Cards *(cont.)*

s	t	u
v	w	x
y	z	

Syllable Walk

Objective: Clapping out syllables

Rationale: An awareness of syllables is an intermediate step leading to phonemic awareness; for many children, hearing syllables in words is easier than hearing individual sounds.

Materials: None

Preparation: None

Procedure:

- Seat the children in a semicircle on the floor or around a small table.

- Tell the students that you are going to listen for syllables in words.

- **Listen to this name.** (Say your first name or use the name Sally if you prefer.) **Can you hear the parts or syllables in my name? Listen again as I say my name and clap for each syllable.**

- **Now I would like you to help me as we say your names and clap out the syllables.**

- Name each child in the group and clap out the syllables. Repeat the activity using last names.

- **Now let's take a walk and clap out the syllables of things around the school.**

- Because syllables build on the foundation of individual words, just work with one word at a time for this introductory syllable activity. Instead of computer room, clap out computer (3). Instead of blue benches, just say and clap out benches (2).

- Possible words include:

door (1)	playground (2)	slide (1)	office (2)
fountain (2)	bathroom (2)	secretary (4)	library (3)
hallway (2)	classroom (2)	gym (1)	principal (3)

- Return to the classroom within the allotted time. Continue naming words in the classroom if time permits.

Syllable Clap

Objective: Counting syllables

Rationale: This is a hands-on review of syllables.

Materials: Basket filled with small objects

Preparation: None

Procedure:

- Seat children on the floor or around a table.

- Ask a volunteer to take one item out of the basket and place it in the center of the group.

- **What did you choose?**

- Help the student with identification, if necessary. Students may identify some items with alternate words (puppy for dog). Accept what is said if it fits the item, and clap out the syllables for that word.

- **Say the word again and clap for each syllable. How many syllables does it have?**

- As the student responds, congratulate or help him/her.

- **Now let's all say the word and clap out the syllables for it.**

- Continue the activity around the group until all items have been used.

- Repeat if time permits. Encourage students to choose different items.

Syllable Board Game

Objective: Clapping the number of syllables in a word

Rationale: Awareness of syllables will be reinforced through a game.

Materials: Picture cards (pages 36–38), game pieces or markers, a game board for each player (page 35)

Preparation: Color and laminate the syllable picture cards if desired, then cut them apart. If you want more cards, you can use picture cards from other sources; or you can make additional cards by using clip art or by cutting pictures from magazines and mounting them on tag. Make one copy of the game board for each player, or substitute one large, blank game board.

Procedure:

- Seat the students at a table or on the floor. Give each student a game board. If you are using one game board, place it in the middle. The syllable cards should be in the center of the group.

- Let each child choose a game piece or marker to place on Start.

- **Today we're going to play a game using syllables. When you draw a card, you will tell us the name of the picture and clap out the syllables. You can then move your game piece or marker that many spaces.**

- Direct a student to begin. Explain the process step by step, if necessary, and assist in clapping out syllables if help is needed.

- Repeat the process with the next student. Continue around the group.

- If you need more cards, mix up the used cards and continue.

- If time permits, begin the game again. If there isn't enough time to complete the game, the student who is closest to the finish is the winner.

The Syllable Game!

Start

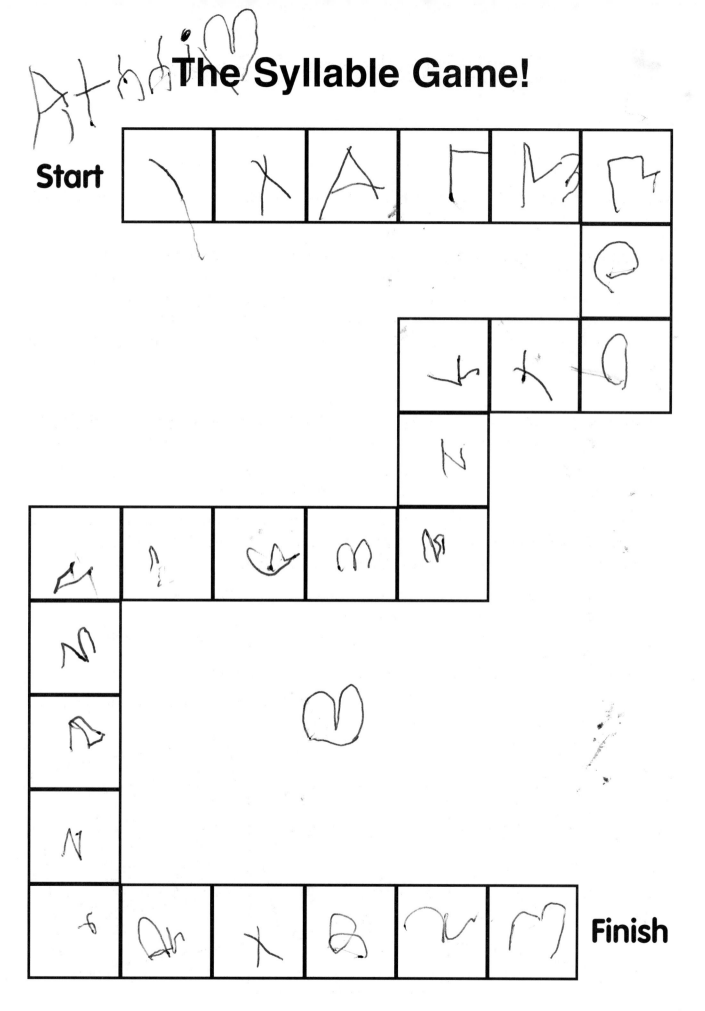

Finish

Syllable Picture Cards

monkey

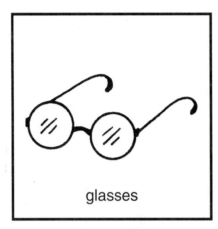

glasses

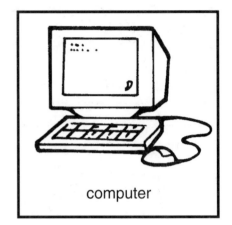

computer

tiger

violin

iguana

apple

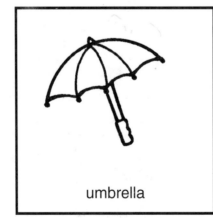

umbrella

elephant

Syllable Picture Cards *(cont.)*

bird

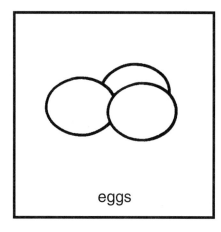
eggs

sun

hat

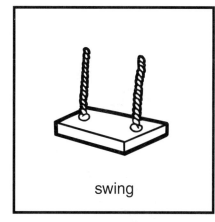
swing

king

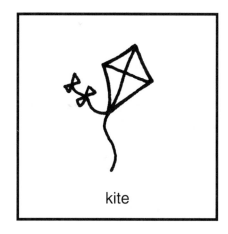
kite

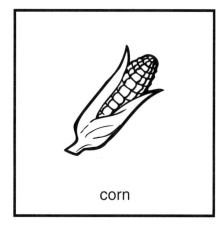
corn

cloud

horse

queen

wagon

Syllable Picture Cards *(cont.)*

kangaroo

butterfly

alligator

tree

banana

ballerina

motorcycle

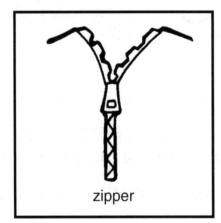

zipper

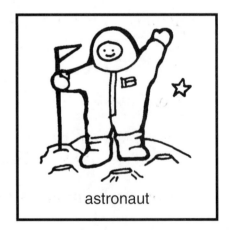

astronaut

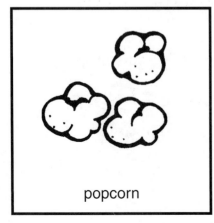

popcorn

watermelon

hippopotamus

Syllable Counting

Objective: Identifying the number of syllables in a word

Rationale: Awareness of syllables will be reinforced by grouping picture cards together according to the number of syllables in each word.

Materials: A pocket chart, picture cards (use the syllable picture cards from the Syllable Board Game, pages 36–38), and number cards for 1–5

Preparation: If number cards are not available, cut out 5 squares and write on them the numbers 1, 2, 3, 4, and 5. Laminate if desired.

Procedure:

- Place the numbers 1, 2, 3, 4, and 5 at the top of a pocket chart. Seat the children in front of the chart. Direct the first child to draw a card.

- **What picture did you draw? Say the word and clap the syllables. How many syllables does it have? Find the number and put your card under it.**

- **Now let's all say the word and clap out the syllables. Was she/he right?**

- Turn to the next child. **Now it's your turn to draw a card.**

- Let the second child complete each step independently if possible. After the card is placed under the correct number, have the group repeat the word and clap out the syllables.

- Continue until you have used all cards.

- **How many picture cards have one syllable? Let's count. How many have two syllables? three syllables? four syllables? five syllables?**

- **Which column has the most cards? Which column has the least?**

- **Let's say all of the one-syllable words again.** Clap as you say each word, following from top to bottom.

- Repeat for all two-syllable words, then for each of the remaining columns.

- If time permits, take down the cards and repeat the entire activity. Encourage students to choose different cards this time.

Alphabet Hunt

Objective: Finding letters in the environment

Rationale: Awareness of alphabet in the environment is a critical pre-reading skill.

Materials: A pencil and a small clipboard with paper attached for each student (A journal or a notebook can be substituted for the clipboard.)

Preparation: None

Procedure:

- Seat the children at a table.

- **Today we are going on a letter hunt. I will give each of you a clipboard with notepaper. Then, we will begin our walk around the school, stopping to write the letters we see along the way.**

- Give each student a clipboard and a pencil.

- Begin the hunt in the classroom, and then move into the hallway. Point out letters along the way. Help students identify letters and allow time to write the letters on the clipboards.

- Move to different locations throughout the school. Some suggestions include the principal's office, kitchen, gym, workroom, secretary's office, etc.

- Return to the room within the allotted time.

Variation: At another time, take clipboards or journals outside. Hunt for letters around the school block or neighborhood. Encourage students to try this activity at home, also.

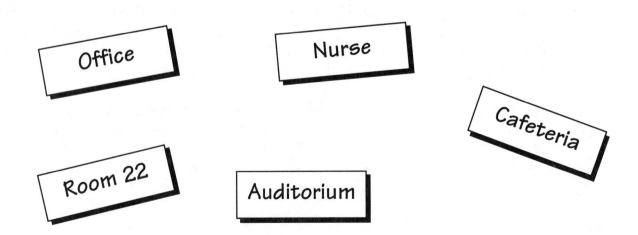

Oddity Rhyming Strips

Objective: Identification of rhyming words

Rationale: By comparing and contrasting pictures, students will practice identifying rhyming sounds.

Materials: Blank rhyming strips (page 42), rhyming picture cards (pages 43–44), completed oddity rhyming strips, glue

Preparation: Copy two blank oddity strip pages for each student plus extra pages for your examples. Copy each rhyming picture card page for every student, plus extra pages for your examples. Then, make four to six completed strips to use as examples. To do this, cut your extra copies of page 42 into strips and cut apart the rhyming picture cards. Next, glue (in any order) two rhyming pictures and one non-rhyming picture on each strip.

Procedure:

- Seat the children at a table. Show them one of your prepared oddity rhyming strips.

- **Today I am going to show you several strips with three pictures. Two of the pictures will rhyme, and the other will be a trick picture, as it does not rhyme with the other two. Okay, let's begin.**

- **Name the pictures with me. _____, _____, and _____. (Student's name), which picture does not rhyme? Great! _____ and _____ are rhyming words, so the _____ is the trick picture.**

- Continue with the other picture strips. Have the students name the rhyming pairs and identify the trick picture.

- **Now we are going to make our own rhyming strips. I will give you each some rhyming pictures and some oddity strips. We will look at the pictures to see if we can find a rhyming pair to glue on one of your strips. After we have glued on a rhyming pair, we will then add a trick picture to your strip.** Pass out the pages and assist the students as they make oddity rhyming strips.

- Continue making strips until the allotted time is up. **Take your rhyming strips home; see if your family can find which two pictures rhyme for each strip.**

Rhyming Strips

Oddity Rhyming Picture Cards

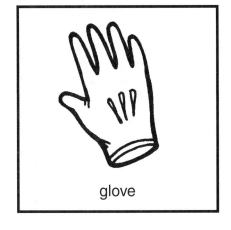

glove

dove

house

mouse

hook

book

lock

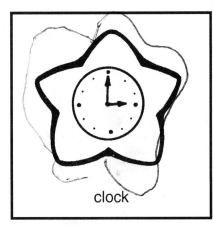

clock

moon

spoon

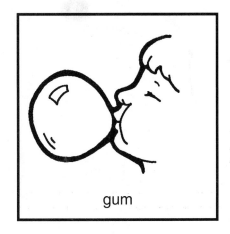

gum

drum

Oddity Rhyming Picture Cards *(cont.)*

skirt

shirt

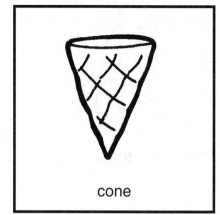

cone

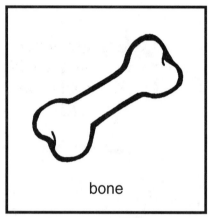

bone

mat

rat

truck

duck

pen

hen

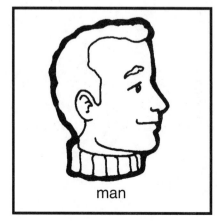

man

pan

Rhyming Odd Man Out

Objective: Identifying rhyming words

Rationale: The skill of rhyming will be reinforced as students compare and contrast objects.

Materials: Rhyming objects (substitute pictures if necessary), a box or a basket

Preparation: Collect rhyming objects for the basket.

Procedure:

- Seat the children at a table.

- **Today we are going to play a rhyming game called Odd Man Out. I am going to pull three objects out of the box. Two of the objects will rhyme, and one will not rhyme. We will call the non-rhyming object the odd man out. This means that he will not belong with the rhyming pair.**

- Pull three objects from the box. Two of these objects need to rhyme; one needs to have a different ending sound.

- **I will put my hand above each object. Say each name with me. _____, _____, and _____.**

- **Which two rhyme? That's right. So, _____ is the odd man out.**

- Do this several times with each child around the circle. When they are familiar with the pattern of the game, they are ready to move on to act as the teacher.

- **Now it is your turn to be the teacher. (Student's name), pull out three items from the box. You need to choose two that rhyme, and one that is different.**

- Assist the student as he or she selects the two rhyming pairs and the odd man out.

- **Great! You now have three items. Let's name them. _____, _____, and _____. Which two rhyme? Which is the odd man out?**

- Continue around the table. Allow each student several turns as the teacher. Give assistance, if necessary, as the students choose their three objects so that only two of the items rhyme, leaving the third item to be the odd man out.

Rhyming Starter Strips

Objective: Identifying rhyming words

Rationale: Awareness of the sounds heard in words is an essential skill for learning to read. This lesson is a hands-on experience with rhyming words.

Materials: A pocket chart, rhyming picture cards (21–23) rhyming starter cards (pages 47–48), starter strips (page 42)

Preparation: A starter strip has a picture followed by two blank spaces. Make six copies of page 42 and cut out the strips. Cut out the rhyming starter cards. Glue each rhyming starter card onto the first square of a strip or simply put the strip in the pocket chart and place the starter card over the first square. Consider laminating the strips and cards for durability.

Procedure:

- Seat the children in front of a pocket chart.

- **Take a look at some cards with me. Let's name the pictures together.**

- Allow the students to handle and examine the pictures. You will need to prompt the students with the intended rhyming word. For example, a picture may need to be called a dog, not a puppy, for rhyming purposes.

- **Today we are going to play a game with these picture cards. First, I will show you the starter strip.**

- Place a starter strip in the pocket chart, and identify the picture in square one.

- **The first picture on our starter strip is _____. Who can think of some words that rhyme with _____? Great, you thought of a lot of words that rhyme with _____. Now let's find the picture cards that rhyme to finish off this strip.**

- A student should find a rhyming card and place it on one of the blank spaces on the starter strip. Have another student find a second rhyming picture for this strip. Be careful to have the students take turns to allow even the quiet students a chance.

- Repeat this procedure with the next starter strip and follow this procedure until you have all of the starter strips in the pocket chart.

- **We've completed all of our rhyming strips; now let's name the pictures for each strip to see if we have all of them with their rhyming sets.**

Rhyming Starter Cards

coat

block

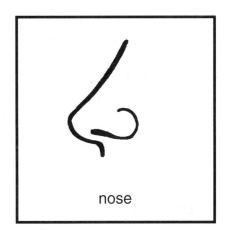

nose

rat

dice

hog

nun

blouse

dock

Rhyming Starter Cards *(cont.)*

key

top

pear

jar

mug

wing

ox

fan

can

Rhyme Time Game

Objective: Producing rhyming words

Rationale: The skill of producing rhyming words will be reinforced as students play the game Rhyme Time.

Materials: Rhyme Time game board (page 50), a place marker for each player, a number die

Preparation: Copy one game board for each student. A large commercial game board may be substituted if you wish to do this as a group activity.

Procedure:

- Seat the children at a table. Give them each a game board.

- **Today we are going to play a rhyming game called Rhyme Time! Everyone needs to choose a place marker and put it on the word *start*.**

- **We will take turns throwing the die and moving a marker along the game board path the number of spaces that match the die.**

- **When you land on a space, tell me the name of the picture and a word that rhymes with the picture name. For example, If you land on a picture of a plane, tell me the word *plane* and a word that rhymes with it, such as rain. If you know a rhyming pair, you can advance one space. If the rhyming pair gives you trouble, you will stay on the place you have landed.**

- Accept nonsense words if they rhyme.

- **We will continue playing the game until someone reaches the word finish.**

Variation 1: After naming a rhyming word, challenge the student to generate one or two more rhymes for the same picture. The student can then advance his/her marker forward one, two, or three spaces depending on the number of rhymes he/she was able to generate.

Variation 2: Make a game board for each student; this change makes the activity seem like a new game to many students. (All directions remain the same.)

Note: This game can be played many times because students will land on different spaces with each game.

Rhyme Time

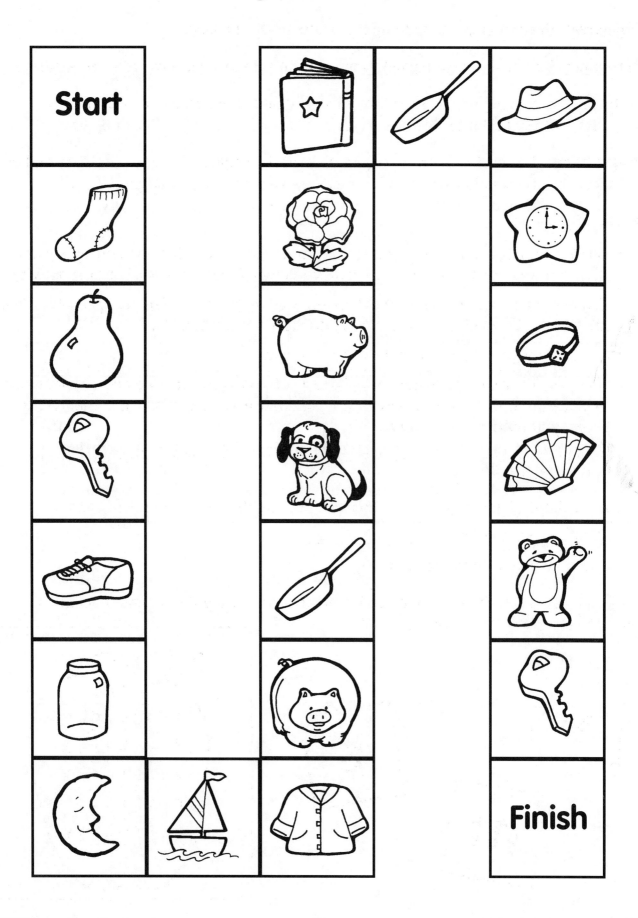

Alphabet Apples

Objective: Recognizing and naming the letters of the alphabet

Rationale: Reviewing the alphabet through a fun activity enhances letter recognition.

Materials: An apple alphabet card for each student (page 52), letter flashcards (pages 29–31)

Preparation: For each player, make one copy of the apple alphabet card. Copy and cut out the letter flashcards from the Alphabet Bingo activity.

Procedure:

- Seat the children at a table. You are the game host! Have fun and convey a game show atmosphere to your group, but stay in control since this is a learning activity.

- **Today we are going to pretend to be on a game show. We're going to play Find the Letter. To begin, I will pass out the apple game boards.**

- Give each "contestant" an apple alphabet board.

- **Now, we are ready to begin. I will draw a letter from the pile and say its name. When I do, find that letter on your apple and touch it! If you are the first to do so, you will win the round.**

- As you draw the card, first say the name of the letter—pause—then show the card to the students.

- After the students have touched the letter, repeat the name of the letter again.

- **That's right, the letter is _____.**

- Continue play as time will allow.

Variation: This activity may be extended another time using the sounds of letters or matching upper and lowercase letters.

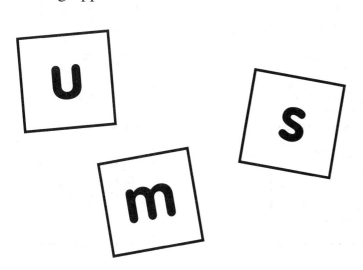

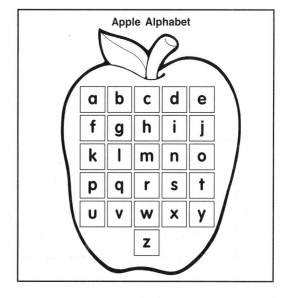

Apple Alphabet

Apple Alphabet

a b c d e
f g h i j
k l m n o
p q r s t
u v w x y
z

Moving with Syllables

Objective: To heighten awareness of syllables through movement

Rationale: Using an action often makes it easier for children to feel and hear the syllables or parts of words.

Materials: None

Preparation: None

Procedure:

- Stand or seat the children around you. **Let's clap together as we break the word** *clapping* **into syllables. Clap…ing. Clap…ing Clap…ing.** Say the word slowly; pause slightly between the syllables. **How many syllables or parts do you hear in** *clapping*?

- **Let's try the word** *hammering*. **Ham…mer…ing. Let's pretend we're hammering into our hands as we beat out the syllables of this word. Ham…mer…ing. Ham…mer…ing. How many syllables do you hear in hammering?**

- Say each of the following words three times while completing a motion for the word. The motion may not fit the meaning of the word, but there must be a separate movement for each syllable. Continue making up motions for the words in the list.

Bow…ing–bend over and stand up.

Tip…toe…ing–take 1 step on tiptoes for each syllable.

March…ing–take 1 marching step for each syllable.

leaning	sewing	wiggling
rolling	shaving	walking
reading	running	snowboarding
roller-skating	stretching	flying
galloping	nodding	saluting
jumping	waving	tapping

Note: If more words are needed, switch to names, months, days of the week, or items around the room. Use a variety of actions (clapping, stamping, nose-tapping, arm-bending, etc.) to emphasize the syllables.

Compound Word Deletion

Objective: Deleting part of a word

Rationale: Awareness of word parts will be reinforced when one part of a compound word is taken away.

Materials: Picture cards that could be part of a compound word (optional)

Preparation: Make or use picture cards you already have. Example: for the word *snowman*, you can use a picture of snow or a picture of a man. For the word *football*, you can use a picture of a foot or a picture of a ball. If you do not have suitable cards, complete this activity orally using the list at the end of the lesson.

Procedure:

- Seat the children at a table.

- **Let's clap out the syllables for snowman. Snow…man. How many syllables do you hear? That's right, snowman has two parts or syllables. In fact, snowman is made up of two words. What are they?**

- **If I take snow away from snowman, what word is left? If I take man away from snowman, what word is left?**

- **Let's clap out the syllables for football. Foot…ball. How many syllables do you hear? What two words do you hear?**

- **If I take foot away from football, what word is left? If I take ball away from football, what word is left?**

- **I'm going to say some more words. When I take one part of the word away, you will have a chance to name the other word.**

- (Skip this line if you are not using pictures.) **We will check your answer with a picture card.**

- **(Student's name), you will be first. If we have the word doghouse and we take the word house away, what will we have left?**

- Give support if necessary by having the group identify the two words in doghouse, then repeat the question.

Compound Word Deletion *(cont.)*

- (Without pictures, say…) **You're right, we would have a dog!**

- (If you are using pictures, say…) **Let's see if you figured out the word. Turn over the top card. Does the picture match the word that you guessed? If we have a doghouse and we take away house, we have a dog!**

- Continue around the table. **If we have the word _____ and we take away _____, what will we have left?**

- Pause for student response. Comment on the student's answer or say, **Let's turn over the next card. Does the picture match the word you guessed?**

- Use words from the following list or develop your own list. Although not all of the suggested words are compound words (e.g. reindeer), they each have two parts that sound like individual words.

popcorn	beehive	bedroom
bluebird	raincoat	skydive
coathook	bookcase	starlight
starfish	seashell	doorbell
sunflower	moonbeam	seagull
teapot	birdseed	meatball
dishwasher	pineapple	reindeer
gingerbread	blackbird	cupcake
Sunday	upstairs	Batman

- As you delete one syllable, vary which part you take away. If you are using pictures, the pictures that you have will determine which part you delete. For example, if you have a picture of an apple, take away *pine* in the word *pineapple*. If you have a picture of a moon, take away *beam* in the word *moonbeam*.

Baker Bob Onset/Rime

Objective: Blending words by onset and rime

Rationale: The onset/rime is an understanding that words are made of sound chunks or segments. The onset is the consonant, digraph, or blend that comes before the rime, and the rime is the vowel and chunk following. The rime is easier for students to hear than individual phonemes.

Materials: Chef-or baker-type puppet, utensils used for cooking, plastic food, table settings, boxes or trays

Preparation: Prepare a box of different items for each child.

Procedure:

• Students should be seated around a table.

• **This puppet is named Baker Bob. He is a great cook! The Baker has one big problem. He can only say words in a special way. He says the first letter or sound separate from the ending chunk. Listen to the way he says my name.**

• Examples: K—athy or Br—enda or Sh—eila. Remember, the onset is the first letter, sound or digraph. The rime starts at the first vowel, and includes everything thereafter.

• **Now, Baker Bob is ready to bake. I am going to give each of you a box full of items that he may need as he cooks. Okay! The first thing he needs is a b—owl. Who has the b—owl?**

• The student with the bowl should respond by holding it up. (Don't expect the student to break up the word. However, you can have her/him say the complete word.)

• **Great! B—owl. (Student's name) has the b—owl.**

• Utensils and plastic food items you may wish to use may include:

f—ork	c—up	sp—oon	kn—ife
pl—ate	wh—ip	l—adle	p—an
gr—ater	m—ixer	f—oil	p—itcher
b—anana	h—amburger	b—utter	fr—ies
p—izza	gr—apes	br—ead	l—ettuce

• Continue to play the game until the boxes are empty or the allotted time runs out.

Alphabet Tree

Objective: Recognizing and naming the letters of the alphabet

Rationale: Connecting the alphabet to a favorite book enhances letter recognition.

Materials: Coconut tree (page 58), letter cards (page 29–31), *Chicka Chicka Boom Boom* (Martin, Bill Jr. and John Archambault. Simon and Schuster Inc., 1989.)

Preparation: None

Procedure:

- Seat the children at a table.

- Show the students the book *Chicka Chicka Boom Boom.* If possible, give each student his or her own copy to follow along.

- **Today I am going to read *Chicka Chicka Boom Boom.* This is a great story about a group of alphabet letters! Listen as I read the story.**

- Read the book.

- **Now we are going to play a game with some letters and a coconut tree.**

- Place the tree in the middle of the group. Put the letters on the table next to the tree.

- **We are going to take turns around the circle. When it is your turn, choose a letter. Tell us the name of the letter and place it on the coconut tree.**

- Begin with the student to your right and continue around the circle.

- If a student does not know the letter, simply tell its name and allow the student to put it on the coconut tree.

Variation 1: Attach the coconut tree to a magnet board and use magnetic letters.

Variation 2: As a challenge, put the letters face down in a pile. Each student will draw the top card and try to identify it when it is his turn.

Coconut Tree

Syllable Deletion

Objective: Deleting part of a word

Rationale: An awareness of word parts will help students later focus on individual sounds within words.

Materials: Multi-syllable objects around the classroom or the school

Preparation: Gather items together or take a walk around the room and/or the school as you did for the Syllable Walk. (Multi-syllable picture cards can be substituted for objects, if you prefer.)

Procedure:

• Seat the children at a table.

• Lay a pencil on the table.

• **Let's clap out the syllables for pencil. Pen…cil. How many syllables do you hear?**

• **If I take pen away from pencil, what's left? If I take cil away from pencil, what word is left?**

• **Let's clap out the syllables for another word.** Point to the alphabet or put an alphabet page on the table. **Al…pha…bet. How many syllables do you hear? If we take away -bet, what's left? If we take away alpha-, what's left?**

• Show the students another object or walk to another item. Have the students identify it and clap out its syllables. Take away one part of the word and have the students name the other part. If students have trouble supplying the word or word part that remains, break the word into its parts together.

• Vary which part of the word you "take away" so students don't always expect to answer with the first or second part of the word.

• After working with compound words and other words that have words within words, continue with two-and three-syllable words that will make nonsense words when broken apart.

Uncle Fred Onset/Rime

Objective: Blending words by onset and rime

Rationale: The onset/rime is an understanding that words are made of sound chunks or segments. The onset is the consonant, digraph, or blend that comes before the rime, and the rime is the vowel and the chunk following. The rime is easier for students to hear than individual phonemes, so it is necessary for them to achieve this skill before segmenting phonemes.

Materials: Farmer Puppet, fence or corral, animals (paper, magnet, or plastic)

Preparation: Divide the animals evenly in prepared totes for your group.

Procedure:

- Students should be seated around a table.

- **Do you remember Baker Bob? Well, today I want to introduce you to his cousin, Fred.**

- **Do you remember the problem that Baker Bob had when he spoke his words?** Responses.

- **He could only say words in a special way. He always said the first letter or sound separate from the ending chunk. Listen to the way he would say his cousin's name. Fr—ed.**

- **Well, Fr—ed has the same problem. Let's see how he says your names.** (Examples: Br—ad, M—andy, D—evin Fr—ank) Remember, the onset is the first letter, sound or digraph. The rime starts with the first vowel, and is everything thereafter.

- **Well, Fr—ed has one thing he really wants to do. He wants to start a farm. He just bought this great big corral, and he needs to find some animals to live in his farm.**

- **That is why he is here today, to see if you can help him.**

- **The first animal he is looking for is a c—ow. Who has the c—ow?**

Uncle Fred Onset/Rime *(cont.)*

- A student will respond by holding up the cow. (Don't expect the student to break up the word. However, you can have her/him say the complete word.)

- **Great! C—ow. (Student's name), has the c—ow!**

- Items or pictures you may wish to use may include:

p-ig	h-orse	k-itten	p-ony
d-uck	g-oat	c-alf	ch-ick
g-oose	h-en	t-urkey	r-ooster
b-ird	l-amb	c-at	d-og
b-unny		sh-eep	p-uppy

- Continue to play the game until the boxes are empty; divide the animals and play again until the allotted time runs out.

Note: Animals other than farm animals may be used, if desired.

What's My Rule? Alliteration

Objective: Developing alliteration skills

Rationale: Student awareness of initial sounds is enhanced with exposure to alliteration. The students will be engaged by manipulating objects.

Materials: Object tubs, at least 5 items for each phoneme featured

Preparation: If possible, include objects for the following "heavy duty" sounds: Ss, Mm, Bb, Hh, Tt, Rr, Ff, Cc, Ww, Pp, and Ll. Remove letter tiles from the tubs since the focus of the lesson is on beginning phonemes.

Procedure:

- Seat the children at a table or on the carpet.

- **Today, we are going to play a game called, What's my Rule? All of the words in this sentence follow a special rule. Listen carefully.**

- **Baby boys bounce balls. Who knows my rule? That is right, all of the words begin with the same sound, b-b-b! B-b-b baby, b-b-b boys, b-b-b bounce, b-b-b balls.**

- **You are doing great! Let's try another sentence. Fabulous Frank found Flora! Who knows my rule?** Listen to the responses and congratulate them for finding the rule. (If per chance a group cannot identify the rule, simply tell them the rule and move on to the next sentence.) Continue the format for the following sentences:

Daisy's doll digs dancing.	Four fish found flowers.
Sam's snake sells sandwiches.	Mighty Mouse made muffins.
Ten turtles tried tacos.	Walter Walrus went walking.
Peggy Pig painted pink pictures.	Rowdy Ryan runs races.

- **Great, you are good at this game! Now we are going to play a different way. I am going to show you a tub with objects. We are going to start with this tub.**

- Choose one at random. **Let's name the objects.** (For example, bat, bee, bug, barn, blue) **Who knows the rule of the tub?** Continue to play with the remaining tubs.

Wee Willie Winkie Alliteration

Objective: Developing alliteration skills

Rationale: Student awareness of initial sounds is enhanced with exposure to alliteration. The students will be engaged by its playful nature.

Materials: A poster of the nursery rhyme "Wee Willie Winkie" (page 64), a wooden or paper frame, large sheets of paper

Preparation: Copy or enlarge the nursery rhyme, "Wee Willie Winkie."

Procedure:

- Seat the children at a table or on the carpet. Show the students the poster of "Wee Willie Winkie."

- **Who can tell me what this poem is about?** Pause and allow student response.

- **Let's read the poem together.** Point to the words as you read.

- **Who can show me the "W" in Wee Willie's name?** Call the students up one at a time to place a frame around the W's.

- **This boy's name is Willie. They have made a new name for him using the W sound, Wee Willie Winkie.** Repeat and exaggerate the initial sound. **/W/—ee W—illie W—inkie.**

- **Today we are going to identify your beginning sound and make a new name for you. Okay, let's start with my name. My name is Kathy. K-k-k-kathy. Who can think of some other words that begin with K-k-k?** (Responses may include cute, cuddly, kicking, kind, kissing, caring, cool; — list the responses on a piece of paper.)

- **Great, we know a lot of words that begin with K-k-k. Now, since we are doing my name, I will choose my two favorite words. I will choose (cute) and (kind). Now my new name will be (cute, kind Kathy).**

- **Now it is time for us to make up a new name for you.** Begin to play the game with the students. Follow the above format for each student's name, listing responses on a separate piece of paper for each child.

- **Now that we all have new names, let's read them together.**

- To further extend, have the students draw a picture of themselves under their new names then bind their work into a book.

Variation: Read "Sing a Song of Sixpence" (page 65) with the students. Exaggerate alliteration as you read and stop to ask students what sound they heard.

Note: This lesson is to reinforce alliteration. Remember, whether the word begins with c or k, g or j, or a vowel, it is the sound of the letter that you will want to use. For example, Austin begins the same as auto or August, but not apple or ant.

Wee Willie Winkie

Wee Willie Winkie runs

through the town,

upstairs and downstairs in his

nightgown.

Rapping on the windows, crying

through the locks,

Are the children in their beds?

For now it's eight o'clock!

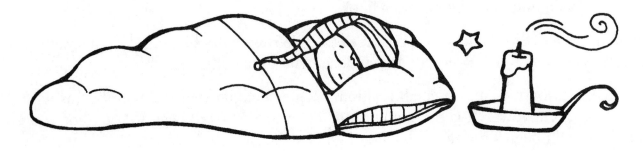

Sing a Song of Sixpence

Sing a song of sixpence,

A pocket full of rye;

Four-and-twenty blackbirds

Baked in a pie!

When the pie was opened

The birds began to sing:

Was not that a dainty dish

To set before the king?

Initial Sound Picture Cards

Objective: Identifying initial phonemes

Rationale: Students need to realize that different words can have the same beginning sound. Particular attention will be paid to how the mouth feels when the sound is made.

Materials: Initial sound picture cards

Preparation: Cut apart the picture cards found on pages 67–73. Consider laminating for durability.

Procedure:

- Seat the children at a table or on the carpet.

- **Today I am going to show you a picture card. As I show you the card, please tell me the name of the picture.**

- Show the pictures one by one, and have the children name the pictures. Make sure that the students are firm on the names of the pictures before continuing the activity.

- **Good job! Now we are going to play a game using these picture cards. I will shuffle the cards and lay them face down in the center of our circle.**

- **We will take turns one by one choosing a card and telling the others in our group the name of the picture.**

- **This might sound easy, but we are going to say the word in a special way. We are going to repeat the beginning sound three times before we say the word.**

- **For example, if you draw a picture of a ball, say the word b-b-b-ball. Then, we will all make the sound, /b-b-b/. Some of us may even know that letter B makes that sound. After we say the sound and the letter, we will look at the picture.**

- Assist students as much as necessary. Give each child an opportunity to draw cards and make the initial sounds.

- Continue to play the game until all the cards are used.

Initial Sound Picture Cards

apple

bee

cat

dinosaur

elephant

fish

gorilla

house

iguana

Initial Sound Picture Cards *(cont.)*

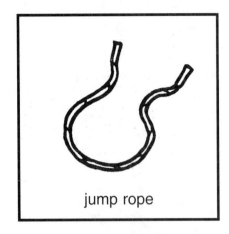

jump rope

kangaroo

lamb

monkey

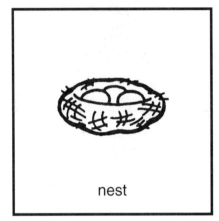

nest

ostrich

pig

queen

robot

sun

tree

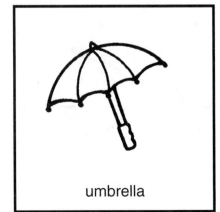

umbrella

Initial Sound Picture Cards *(cont.)*

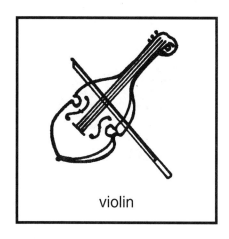
violin

wagon

x-ray

yarn

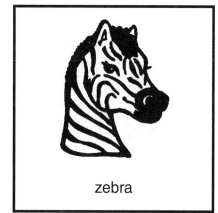
zebra

alligator

bear

cookie

dog

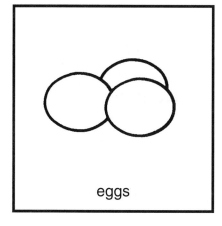
eggs

frog

guitar

Initial Sound Picture Cards *(cont.)*

heart

igloo

jet

king

lion

mouse

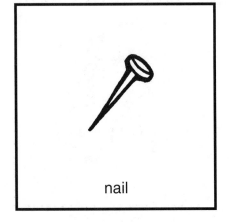

nail

octopus

penguin

quilt

rabbit

snake

Initial Sound Picture Cards *(cont.)*

tiger

unicorn

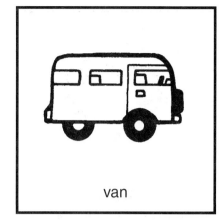

van

whale

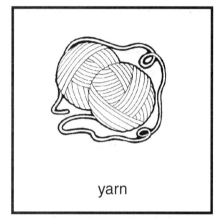

yarn

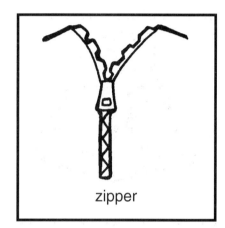

zipper

apple tree

book

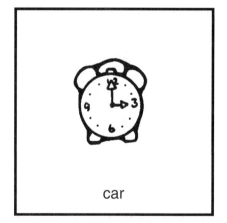

car

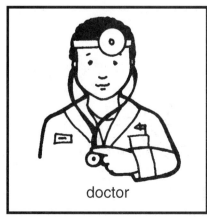

doctor

elf

flag

Initial Sound Picture Cards *(cont.)*

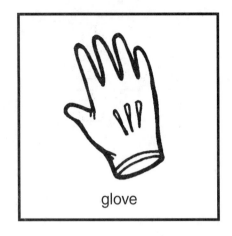

glove

hat

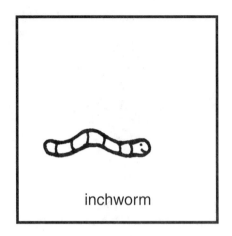

inchworm

Jack-O-Lantern

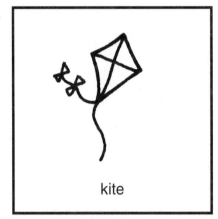

kite

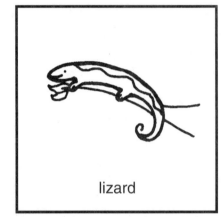

lizard

monkey

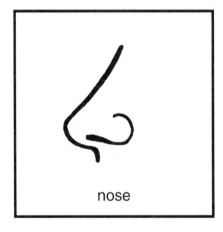

nose

otter

pie

quarter

rocket

Initial Sound Picture Cards *(cont.)*

seahorse

turtle

umpire

volcano

watermelon

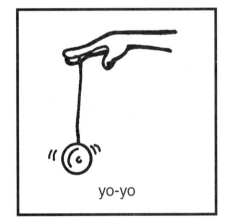

yo-yo

zoo

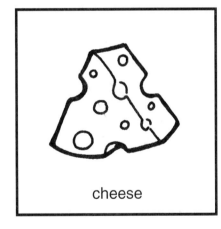

cheese

chimney

shoe

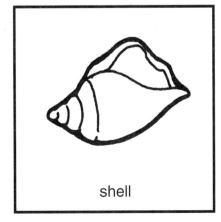

shell

Alphabet Match

Objective: Matching capital and lowercase letters

Rationale: Naming and matching letters in a familiar game format will reinforce letter recognition.

Materials: A set of letter cards including 8–13 of the capital letters and a set of the matching lowercase letter cards.

Preparation: To make cards for this game, use the letter cards from the Alphabet Bingo game, pages 26–31. Copy the capital letter cards on blue paper or tag and the lowercase letters on yellow paper or tag. (You may substitute other colors.) Laminate, if desired, and cut the letters apart.

Procedure:

- Place the cards face down on a table or the floor. Keep all of the capital letters together and all of the lowercase letters together.

- Seat the children around the cards. Direct the first child to draw a blue card.

- **What letter did you draw? What is the sound for that letter?** Have the other players help with the letter and sound, if necessary.

- **Now draw a yellow card. What letter is it? What is the sound for that letter? Do the letters match?**

- If the letters match, let that child keep the pair. If they do not match, turn them over in the same places on the table or floor.

- Turn to the next student. **Now it's your turn to draw a card.**

- Let the second child complete each step. Continue until you have used all cards.

- Make sure you ask each student to identify the letter and the sound for each card drawn.

- If time permits, exchange this set for a different set of capital and lowercase letters.

- If you want to challenge a group, add more letters to one of the sets, or combine sets.

74

I Spy Initial Sounds

Objective: Using initial phonemes in different words

Rationale: The students will practice initial phonemes and realize that different words can have the same beginning sound. Particular attention will be paid to how the sound feels inside the mouth when it is made.

Materials: None

Preparation: None

Procedure:

- Seat the children at a table or on the carpet.

- **Today we are going to play a game called I Spy. We are going to take a walk around our school, stopping at different places to play the game.**

- **Let's begin here in our room. I am thinking of something. I spy something that begins with the sound /c/c/c/. Does anyone have a guess?**

- Allow the children ample opportunity to think of words that begin with the phoneme c before giving the second clue.

- **Great, you have listed a lot of words that begin with the sound /c/c/c/.**

- **Now, here comes clue #2. This thing goes tick tock tick tock. Does anyone have a guess? (Student's name), you are right, I am thinking of a clock.**

- **Now, (student's name), it is your turn. Look around the room and think of an object. When you are ready, give us a clue.**

- Proceed with the child's turn, giving assistance if needed.

- **Okay, let's move to a new spot and play again.**

- Move to locations around the school, playing the game. Try such places as the hall, kitchen, office, workroom, spare classroom, etc. At each location, you choose the first word. Model as you did previously, then let a student try a word. Continue the game for the allotted time.

Initial Sound Wheels

Objective: Matching pictures of like sounds

Rationale: Choosing picture cards of like sounds will reinforce student awareness of beginning sounds.

Materials: One wheel and six pie pieces for each student (pages 77–82), baggies

Preparation: Copy wheels onto tag and laminate, if possible. Cut out the bottom wheel of each page and leave whole; cut the top wheel of each page into six pie pieces. Keep the wheel and the cut pie pieces together (possibly in a baggie) as the students will be matching pictures with like sounds during this game. Do the same for each page of wheels.

Procedure:

- Seat the children in a semi-circle or at a table.

- **Today we are going to name the sound for each picture on our wheels. Each of us will have a different sound wheel, and a baggie of pie shapes with matching sounds. Listen as I show you the pictures on each wheel.**

- Show the pictures one by one on each wheel, and have the children name the pictures. Make sure that the students are firm on the names of the pictures before continuing.

- Demonstrate how the game will be played. Place a wheel in front of you, and draw a pie piece out your baggie. Say the name of the picture on the pie shape, such as flag. Exaggerate the beginning sound and talk about how it feels in your mouth when you say /f/f/f/. Then place the pie on its matching sound picture upon the wheel.

- **The picture *flag* begins the same as *fish*, so I will place my pie shape on the fish.** Place the flag upside down on the wheel so you can definitely see which pictures have been covered. Continue modeling the game for two more pie-shapes.

- **Okay, now it is your turn to play.** Give each student a wheel packet. **Place your wheels in front of you and begin. Remember, I will help you if you get stuck.**

- When every player covers his/her wheel, trade packets and begin again.

Note: Focus on the first letter sound only, even if the word begins with a blend. Identifying the first sound of a blend lays the foundation for segmenting.

Initial Sound Wheels

Cut this wheel apart!

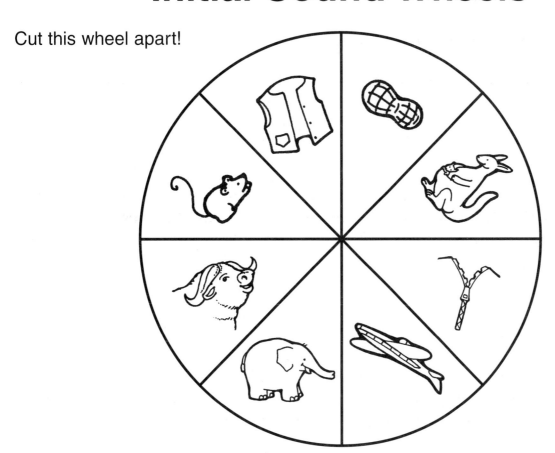

Leave this wheel whole!

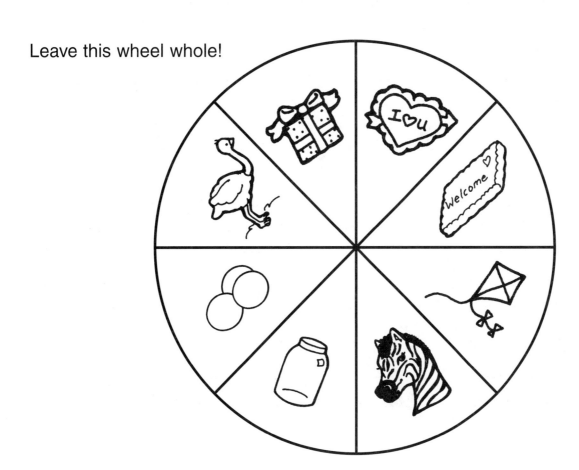

Initial Sound Wheels *(cont.)*

Cut this wheel apart!

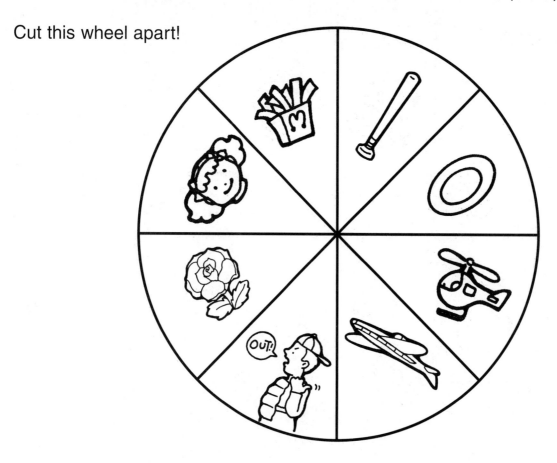

Leave this wheel whole!

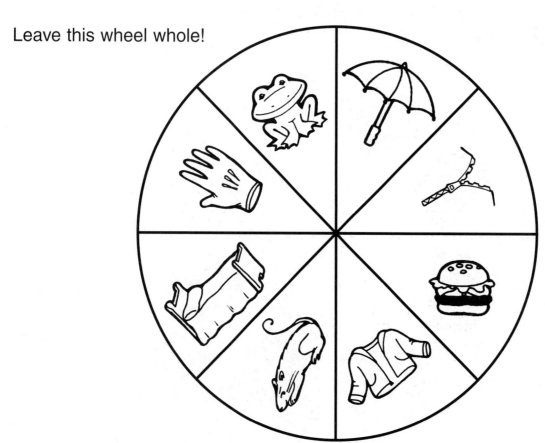

Initial Sound Wheels *(cont.)*

Cut this wheel apart!

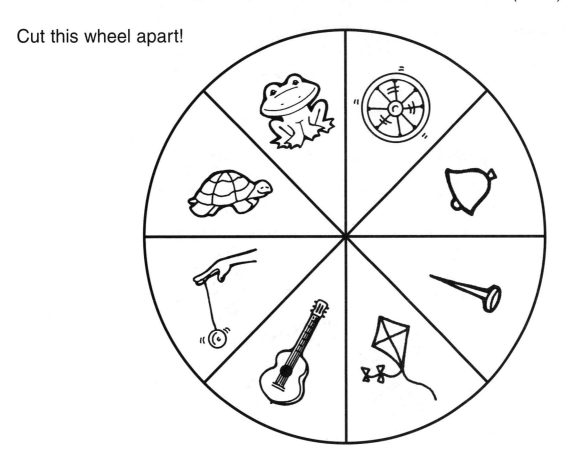

Leave this wheel whole!

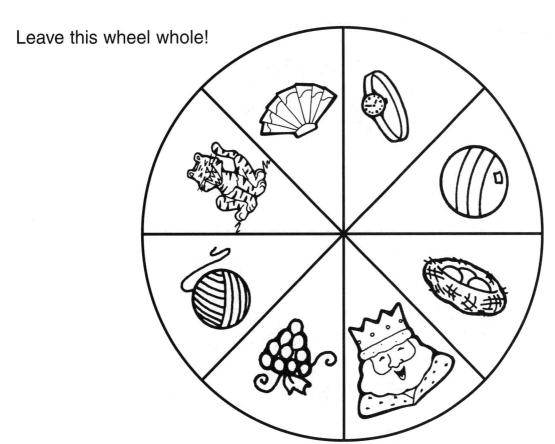

Initial Sound Wheels *(cont.)*

Cut this wheel apart!

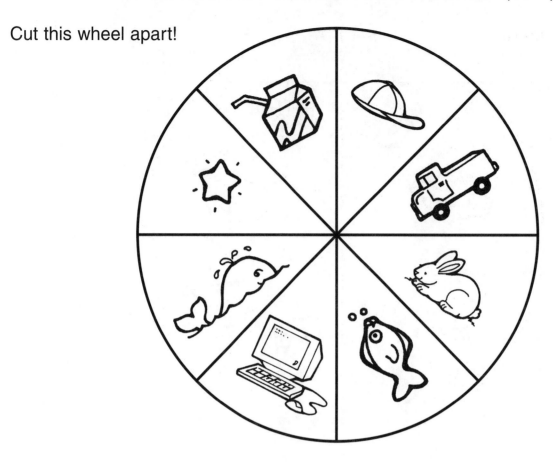

Leave this wheel whole!

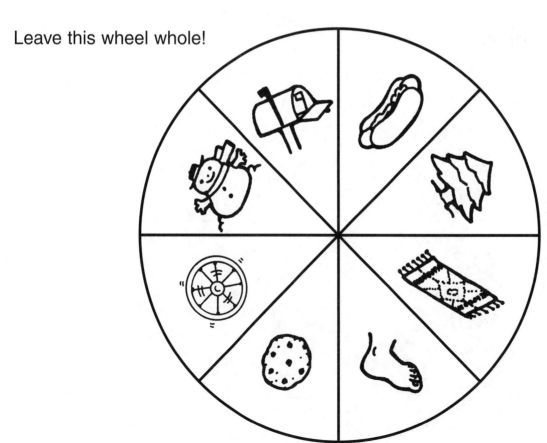

Initial Sound Wheels *(cont.)*

Cut this wheel apart!

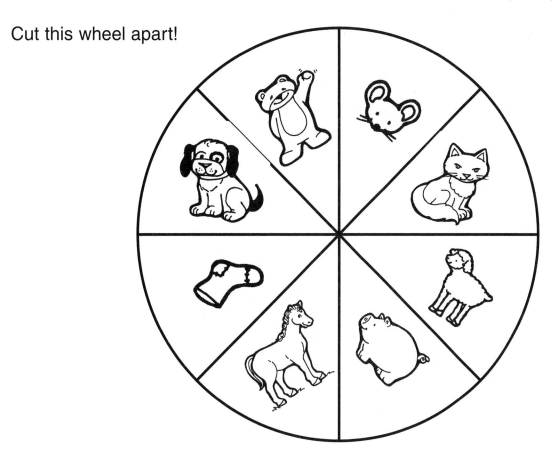

Leave this wheel whole!

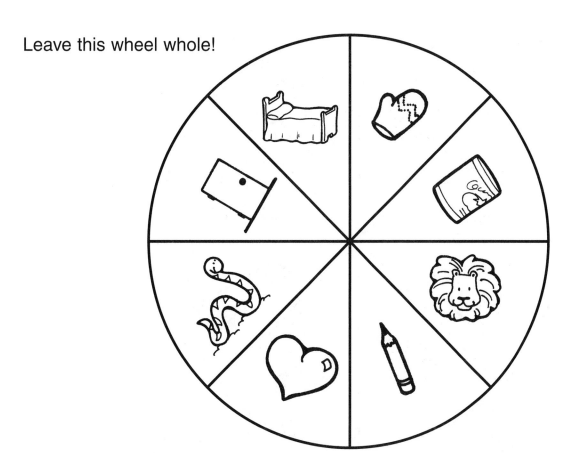

Initial Sound Wheels *(cont.)*

Cut this wheel apart!

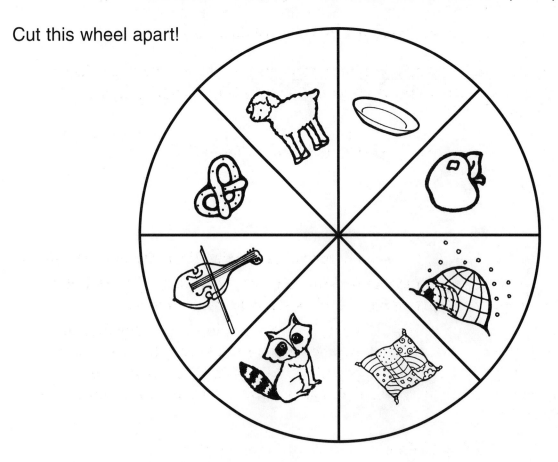

Leave this wheel whole!

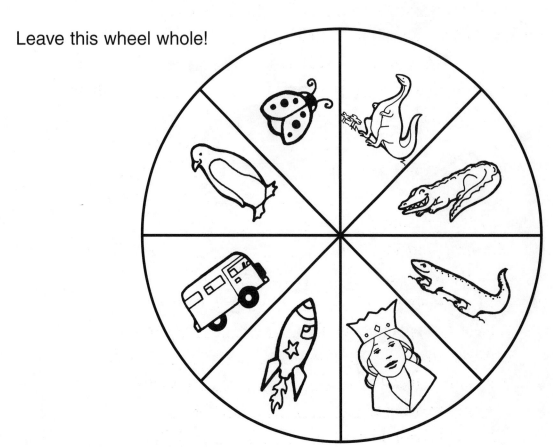

Down by the Bay Rhyming

Objective: Producing a rhyming word that makes sense in a sentence

Rationale: In addition to recognizing rhymes, students need to be able to produce rhymes. This activity provides an opportunity for practicing rhyme production.

Materials: *Down by the Bay* (Raffi. Crown Publishers, Inc., 1987.)

Preparation: None

Procedure:

- Seat the children in a semicircle on the floor or at a table. Read *Down by the Bay*.
- **Let's make up some new *Down by the Bay* rhymes. I'll start. Think before you answer so the word rhymes and makes sense in the sentence.**
- Try the following examples, then make up your own *Down by the Bay* rhymes. Have the entire group work together for the first 4–8 sentences, then try 1 or 2 rounds asking individual children to complete the rhyme. The answers are suggestions only; accept any rhyme that makes sense. Give additional hints, if necessary.

Did you ever see a cat wearing a _____? (hat)

Did you ever see a goat wearing a _____? (coat)

Did you ever see a ball bouncing through a _____? (hall)

Did you ever see a mouse running through a _____? (house)

Did you ever see three kittens wearing some _____? (mittens)

Did you ever see a bug sitting on a _____? (rug)

Did you ever see a bear sitting in a _____? (chair)

Did you ever see a fish swimming in a _____? (dish)

Did you ever see a boat being sailed by a _____? (goat)

Did you ever see a flea chasing a _____? (bee)

Did you ever see a frog hopping over a _____? (dog)

Did you ever see a fly wearing a _____? (tie)

Did you ever see a cat swinging a _____? (bat)

Did you ever see a fox jumping out of a _____? (box)

Did you ever see some mice playing in the _____? (rice)

Did you ever see a bell shaped like a _____? (shell)

Did you ever see a pig wearing a _____? (wig)

Did you ever see a light flying like a _____? (kite)

Snowman Initial Sounds

Objective: Matching pictures to beginning sounds

Rationale: Awareness of beginning sounds will be reinforced through a matching activity.

Materials: (optional) A snowman workmat for each child (page 85), small picture "buttons" (pages 86–87)

Preparation: Copy one snowman to be used as a workmat for each student in the group. Cut out one button per student for each phoneme that you feature. (Color and laminate, if desired, before cutting.) You may need to use some duplicate pictures, depending on the size of your group.

Procedure:

- Seat the children in a semi circle or at a table. Give each child a workmat. Spread out the set of cards so all pictures can be seen.

- **Today we're going to listen to beginning sounds and match pictures to those sounds. Listen to our first sound. /s/, /s/.** Be sure to make the sound; do not say the letter s at this time. **Do you see a picture that starts with that sound? Pick it up while I sing a song.**

- Chant the following words or sing them using the tune of Ten Little Indians.

  Pick up a /s/ card and put it on the snowman.

  Pick up a /s/ card and put it on the snowman.

  Pick up a /s/ card and put it on the snowman.

  What picture did you find?

- If you are not using workmats, substitute "hold it up high" for "put it on the snowman." If you are using another seasonal workmat (e.g. a pumpkin, a Christmas tree), adjust words to fit.

- Turn to the child on your right. **Name the picture that you found. What sound do you hear at the beginning of the word?** Continue around the circle, asking the same questions. **Let's try that again with another sound.**

- Choose another phoneme and sing or chant the song. Repeat the questions. Continue until you have used all the phonemes that you are featuring for this lesson.

Snowman Workmat

Snowman Initial Sounds

Snowman Initial Sounds *(cont.)*

Alphabet Board Game

Objective: Recognizing letters of the alphabet

Rationale: Reviewing the alphabet through a game will enhance letter recognition.

Materials: Alphabet game board for each player, game pieces or markers, number die

Preparation: Make a copy of the alphabet board on page 89 for each player.

Procedure:

- Seat the children around at table or on the floor. Give each student an alphabet game board.

- Have each student choose a game piece and put it on Start.

- **Today we're going to play an alphabet game. (Student's name), you will be first.**

- **Shake the die, then move your marker that many spaces.**

- **What letter did you land on? Do you know the sound for that letter?**

- If the student does not know the letter, let another student whisper its name. Help with sounds, if necessary.

- Continue around the table. If you have time, play the game again. Challenge students (who are able) to name a word beginning with the sound that they land on.

Variation: Make a large game board and put a letter in each space. Follow the same rules.

Alphabet Board Game				
		Bb	Uu	Ww
Start		Tt		Hh
		Ss		Mm
Aa		Rr		Gg
Dd		Xx		Nn
Ff		Ll		
Oo				Finish
Zz	Qq	Ee		

Alphabet Board Game

Start		Bb	Uu	Ww
Aa		Tt		Hh
Dd		Ss		Mm
Ff		Rr		Gg
Oo		Xx		Nn
Zz	Qq	Ll		Finish
		Ee		

I Went for a Walk Rhymes

Objective: Producing rhymes

Rationale: Focusing on word families will enhance awareness of rhymes.

Materials: A beanbag to toss, a whiteboard or chalkboard

Preparation: None

Procedure:

- Seat the children around a whiteboard or a chalkboard. Write *cat* on the board.

- **This is the word *cat*. Who can name a rhyme for cat?** Write the rhymes that the students name.

- **We are going to play a game using the rhyming words for cat. I'll start the game. I went for a walk and I saw a cat.**

- Toss the beanbag to a student. **What did you see on your walk?**

- Help the student pick out a rhyming word from the list and repeat the phrase "I went for a walk and I saw a...." He/she should then toss the beanbag back to you.

- **Yes, cat and _____ rhyme.**

- Toss the beanbag to another student. **What did you see on your walk?**

- Repeat the above step. Help as much as necessary. Say the rhyme each time. When the students run out of rhymes for cat, make a rhyme for a new word and continue the game. Choose from the following suggestions, then add your own words.

  I went for a walk and I saw a dog. (log, hog, frog)

  I went for a walk and I saw a fair. (bear, chair, pear)

  I went for a walk and I saw a bee. (pea, key, tree)

  I went for a walk and I saw a man. (can, fan, pan, van)

Variation: Instead of taking a walk, try this sentence near Christmas.

  The tree is covered with stars. (cars, jars)

  The tree is covered with bears. (pears, chairs)

Roll and Rhyme

Objective: Generating rhyming words

Rationale: Generation is a high level of rhyming that helps prepare students for phoneme manipulation. Students will practice generating rhymes through this kinesthetic activity.

Materials: A ball, a nursery rhyme book

Preparation: None

Procedure:

- Seat the students in a circle on the floor.

- **Today we are going to play a game with rhyming words. We will need this ball to roll around in our circle. Let's practice rolling the ball to anyone we choose.**

- Allow ample opportunity to practice rolling the ball in the circle.

- **Great, we are terrific at rolling!**

- **Now we are going to add an even harder step. We are going to recite a nursery rhyme, but we will pause when we get to a special rhyming word. That is when we will begin to roll the ball as we make up some new rhymes. Okay, let's try it.**

- Recite "Jack and Jill" together.

  Jack and Jill went up the hill

  To fetch a pail of water,

  Jack fell down and broke his crown,

  And Jill came tumbling after.

- Repeat the nursery rhyme, pausing when you get to hill this time.

- **Now we are going to roll the ball and name a new word that rhymes with hill.**

- Have the child who is holding the ball at that time give a rhyming word such as pill. Then he or she will roll it to another who will give yet another rhyme such as will.

- After four or five rhyming words are generated, begin again with a new nursery rhyme.

Photo Initial Sounds

Objective: Isolating the beginning phoneme

Rationale: This lesson is designed to give students practice isolating the initial sound or beginning phoneme of familiar words.

Materials: A picture or photograph of each student

Preparation: Take a picture of each student.

Procedure:

- Seat the children at a table. Show the students the cards with pictures of their classmates.

- **Today we are going to play a game using the names of our classmates. I am going to place the cards in a pile, and we will take turns drawing cards.**

- Place cards in a pile in the center of the table.

- **I will go first.** (Draw a card) **Okay, guess whose name I'm going to say. Listen carefully. I have a picture of /d/d/d/d/.** Repeat the phoneme over and over, clearly and distinctly. If it is a continuant consonant such as m or s, stretch the sound as well as repeat it, such as /sssss/sssss/ssss/ or /mmmmm/mmmmmm/mmmmmm/.

- **Does anyone have a guess?** Allow students to guess the name.

- **The name is _____.** (Show them the picture card as you say the name.)

- If more than one child's name has the same initial sound, encourage the children to guess all of the possibilities.

- **Okay, (Student's name), now it is your turn.**

- Continue the game until all of the picture cards have been used. Assist as much as necessary.

- **You are great at beginning sounds!**

- Shuffle the cards and play the game again until the allotted time is up.

Initial Sounds Object Oddity

Objective: Identifying items with matching initial sounds

Rationale: Oddity activities help students focus on similarities and differences. Determining which items belong together will reinforce initial sounds.

Materials: A basket of small objects

Preparation: Gather objects for the basket.

Procedure:

- Seat the children in a semi circle or at a table. Choose two items beginning with the same sound and a third item with a different initial sound.

- Name each item as you set it on the table or floor.

- **(Student's name), which two items go together? What sound do you hear at the beginning of each word?** Allow other students to help, if necessary.

- **Which item is the odd man out? What sound do you hear at the beginning of (name object)?**

- Set the three items aside. Choose three new objects and repeat the process.

- Continue activity throughout allotted time. If all objects are used, begin again with different combinations.

Initial Sounds Picture Oddity

Objective: Matching and identifying beginning sounds

Rationale: The ability to identify beginning phonemes will be reinforced as students match cards beginning with the same sound.

Materials: Pocket chart, a set of picture cards

Preparation: Use a commercial set of pictures or the initial sound cards found on pages 67–73. Arrange the pictures so two in every set of four begin with the same sound.

Procedure:

- Seat the students in front of the pocket chart. **I'm going to put some pictures in the pocket chart. We will try to match the sound of the first card with one other card in the same row.** Put up the first card, naming it as you put it on the chart. Put up and name three more cards in the same row, going left to right.

- **Listen to the first sound of (name the first picture). Which picture begins with the same sound as (name first picture)?**

- The student answering the question should come up and point to the matching picture. Name each picture again, if necessary.

- **That's right! What sound do you hear at the beginning of _____ and _____?**

- Remember, focus on the sound, not the letter making the sound. If a student names the letter, be sure to ask the student to name the sound, also.

- (If the wrong sound is given, say the following.) **What sound do you hear at the beginning of (name the first picture)? What sound do you hear at the beginning of (name the picture the student chose)? Are they the same? Listen as I say all four picture names again; which picture begins with the same sound as (name the first picture)?**

- Continue adding four pictures per pocket-chart row. Vary the placement of the matching card so it is not always in the same location. Repeat the activity if you make it through all of the cards. This time, have the students identify all four beginning sounds after naming the two matching cards.

Strip Picture Initial Sounds

Objective: Matching and identifying beginning sounds

Rationale: The ability to identify beginning phonemes will be reinforced as students match pictures beginning with the same sound.

Materials: Picture strips

Preparation: To make picture strips, cut tag into strips and put four stickers in a row on the strip. The first sticker should match one of the remaining three stickers.

Procedure:

- Seat the students around a table. Place strips face down on the table.

- Take a picture strip. **Look at the pictures on my strip; name them with me.**

- **Listen to the first sound in (name the first picture). Which of these begins with the same sound as (name the first picture)?**

- **You're right! _____ and _____ both begin with the _____ sound.** Point to the matching pictures as you say the names.

- Turn to the child sitting next to you. **(Student's name), choose a strip. Let's name the pictures together.** Name the pictures left to right as you point to each one.

- **Which picture begins with the same sound as (name of first picture)? That's right! What sound do you hear at the beginning of _____ and _____?**

- Remember to focus on the sound, not the letter making the sound. If a student names the letter, be sure to ask the student to name the sound, also.

- (If the wrong sound is given, say the following.) **What sound do you hear at the beginning of (name the first picture)? What sound do you hear at the beginning of (name the picture the student chose)? Are they the same? Listen as I say all four picture names again; which picture begins with the same sound as (name the first picture)?**

- Have the next child take a picture strip and repeat the procedure. Continue around the group until you have used all picture strips. If time permits, mix up the strips and begin again.

Wiggle Eye Alphabet

Objective: Recognizing letters of the alphabet

Rationale: Reviewing the alphabet through a game will enhance letter recognition.

Materials: A small alphabet page and a wiggle eye pointer for each student

Preparation: For each student make a copy of the alphabet on page 52. A wiggle eye pointer is made by gluing a wiggle eye to the end of a craft stick.

Procedure:

- Seat the students at a table and give each child an alphabet page.

- **Today we're going to play an alphabet game. We're going to name alphabet letters and point to them. I'll start.**

- **I spy with my wiggle eye the letter *m*. Everyone, find the letter *m* on your alphabet page. Point to it with your wiggle eye. Do you know what sound m makes?**

- **Let's try that again. (Student's name), you will be next. Name a letter. Say, "I spy with my wiggle eye the letter _____."**

- **Everyone, find the letter _____ on your alphabet page and point to it with your wiggle eye. Do you know what sound _____ makes?**

- Continue around the group as long as time permits.

Variation 1: Point to letters in books or to letters around the room.

Variation 2: Use one long pointer and a large central alphabet chart instead of individual pointers and charts.

Initial Sounds Starter Strips

Objective: Matching like initial sounds

Rationale: Discriminating matching initial sounds is a critical pre-reading skill.

Materials: Initial sound starter strips (pages 98–105), initial sounds picture cards (pages 67–73), pocket chart (optional)

Preparation: Cut out the initial sound starter strips. Laminate, if desired.

Procedure:

- Seat the children at a table or in front of a pocket chart.

- Choose eight starter strips to begin working with immediately. Show the students the picture cards for those strips and ask them to identify the pictures. You may occasionally need to prompt them with the intended words. For example, students may identify the sea as the ocean or beach. In this case, tell them they're right, but there is also another name for it that starts with /s/. Ask if anyone knows the name; if not; simply tell them your intended name for the picture card.

- Once the students are familiar with the picture cards, spread them out so all pictures can be seen.

- Lay the starter strip for /b/ on the table or put it in a pocket chart.

- Point to the boat at the beginning of the strip. **What is this picture?**

- **Right, it is a boat. Who can tell me the sound** (remember to use the word *sound*, not the word *letter*) **of the word boat?**

- Have the students look at the picture cards and find other items that start with the /b/ sound. Continue until all of the blank spaces are covered or until all of the cards for /b/ have been found.

- **These pictures start with /b/. Let's name all of the pictures on this strip together. Listen closely to the beginning sound of each word.**

- Repeat this activity with the rest of the starter strips. Change starter strips and picture cards after completing the first set of eight, then repeat the process.

Initial Sound Starter Strips

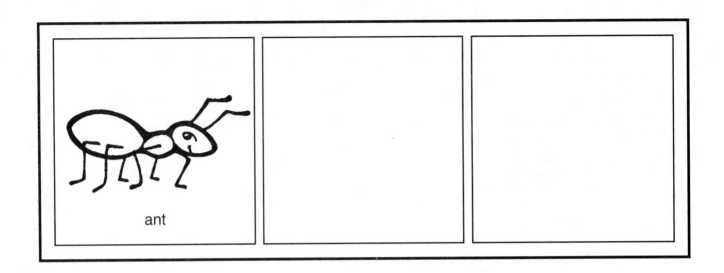

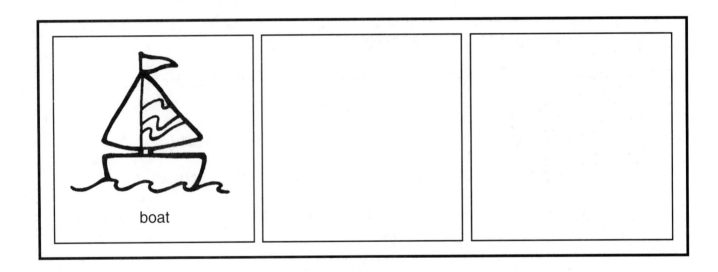

Initial Sound Starter Strips *(cont.)*

duck

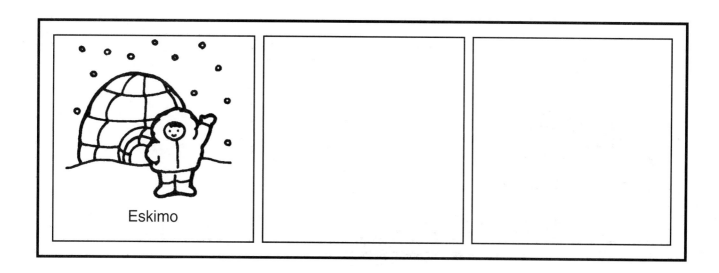

Eskimo

fan

Initial Sound Starter Strips *(cont.)*

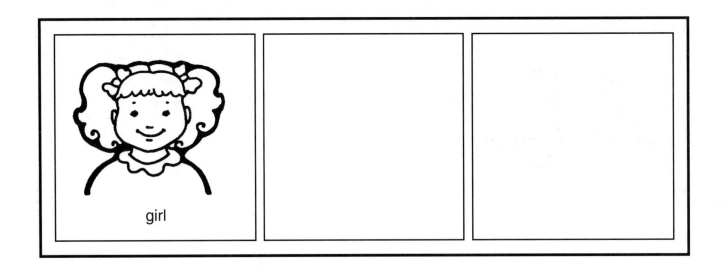

girl

hand

insect

Initial Sound Starter Strips *(cont.)*

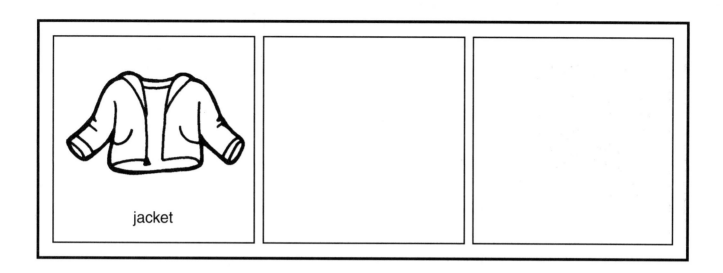

jacket

kitten

ladder

Initial Sound Starter Strips *(cont.)*

moon

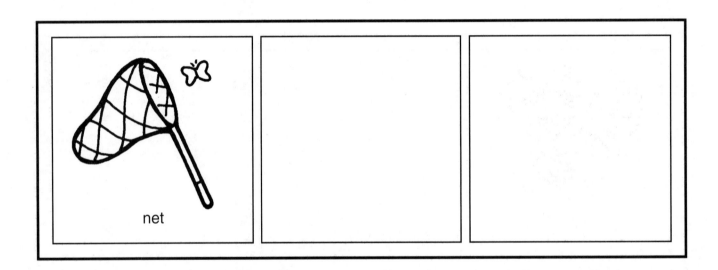

net

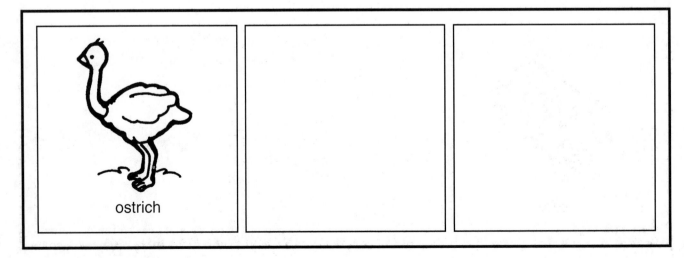

ostrich

Initial Sound Starter Strips *(cont.)*

quail

raccoon

soap

Initial Sound Starter Strips *(cont.)*

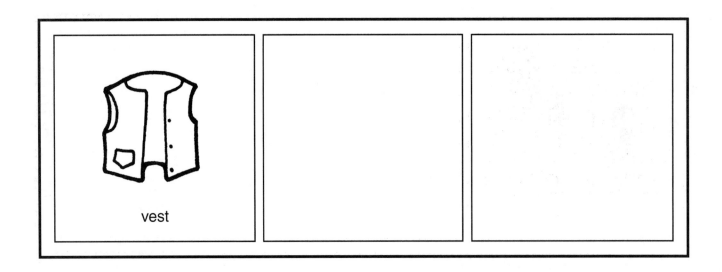

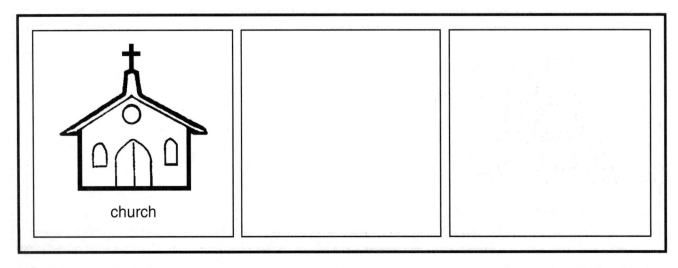

Initial Sound Starter Strips *(cont.)*

yak

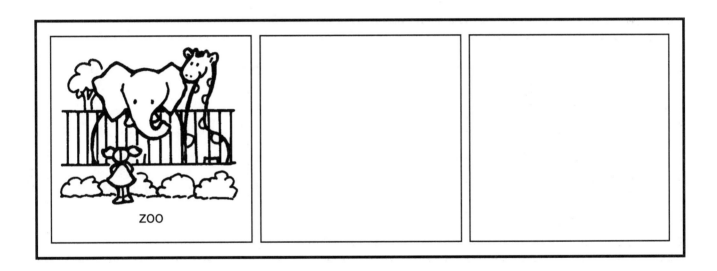

zoo

ship

Initial Sounds Objects

Objective: Isolating the beginning phoneme

Rationale: The students need adequate practice identifying the beginning sound of familiar words. This is an important pre-reading skill.

Materials: A cookie sheet, tray, or box, and several items, each beginning with a different sound

Preparation: Find and place the items on the tray.

Procedure:

- Seat the children at a table.

- **Today we are going to play a game using the objects on this tray.**

- Place the tray with objects in the center of the table. Name the objects as you point to them.

- **I will go first. Guess what I am spying. It begins like this /d/d/d/d/d/d/d/. Does anyone have a guess?**

- **(Student's name), you are right. You may take the object and place it in front of you.**

- Continue taking turns with this game, replacing items on the tray as needed, then replaying until time runs out.

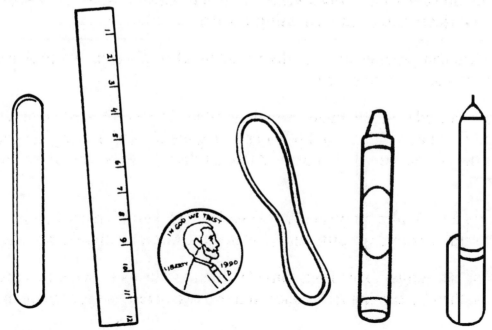

Rhyming Game

Objective: Producing and generating rhymes

Rationale: Students who can produce and generate rhymes can more readily understand phoneme manipulation. This game will provide an opportunity for rhyming practice.

Materials: Blank game board for each student (page 108), game pieces or markers, number die, objects, basket

Preparation: Copy a gameboard for each student. Gather the objects and place them in the basket. Picture cards may be substituted for the objects, if necessary.

Procedure:

- Seat the children around a table; give each student a game board. (A large game board can be substituted for the individual boards.) Have each student choose a game piece and put it on Start.

- **Today we're going to play a rhyming game. (Student's name), you will be first. Draw an object out of the basket. Make up a rhyming word for (name object).**

- If the student cannot name a rhyme, let another student whisper a rhyming word; a rhyming word must be named before the student can move his/her game piece. Accept nonsense words if they rhyme.

- **You're right! _____ rhymes with (name object). Shake the die, then move your marker that many spaces. Can you name another rhyming word for (name object) and (name rhyming word)?**

- If the student can generate another rhyme, let him/her move one more space. Do not offer assistance for this step.

- Set the object aside and continue around the table. Have each student draw an object and name a rhyming word before shaking the die and moving the game piece. If the student can generate an additional rhyme, he/she can move one more space.

- If you have time, return all objects to the basket and play the game again. Challenge students to draw different objects and come up with new rhyming words.

Variation: You can further extend the game by asking students to name two additional rhyming words, thereby earning the chance to move two additional spaces on the game board.

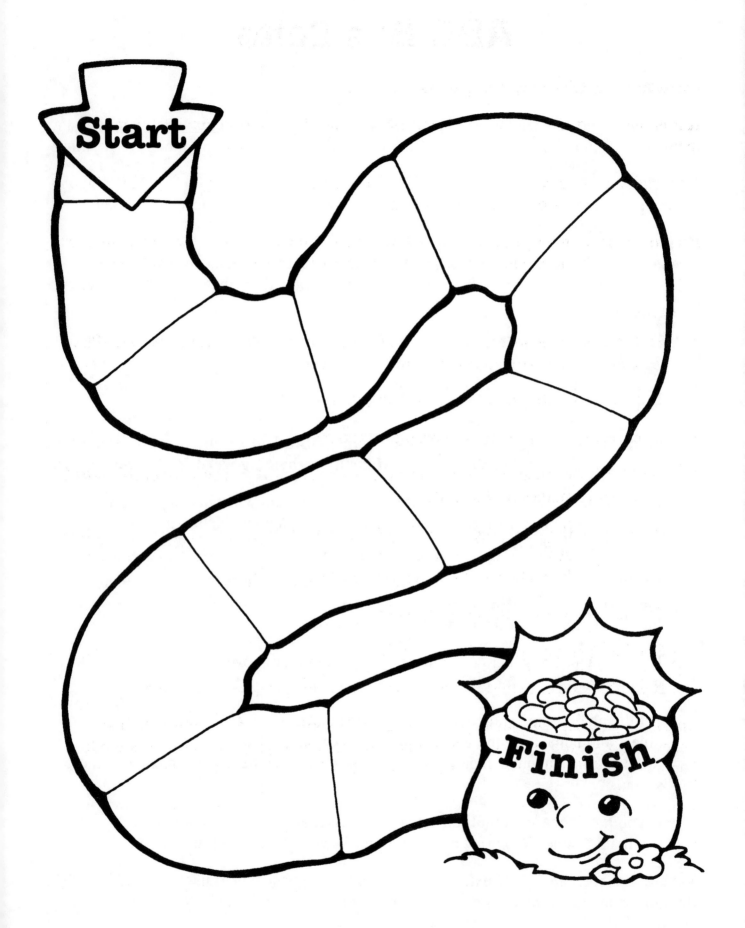

ABC Bus Lotto

Objective: Matching beginning sounds to letters

Rationale: Students need to be able to connect sounds with the letters that represent them.

Materials: Picture cards (pages 67–73), a bus card for each student (110–112), Bingo markers or some kind of counter

Preparation: Run the bus cards on yellow tag and laminate, if possible; cut them apart. Choose initial sound picture cards to match the letters on each bus.

Procedure:

- Seat students around a table or on the floor and give each student a bus card. Place the picture cards face up in the center.

- **Today we're going to match beginning sounds to letters.**

- Direct a student to begin by choosing a picture card.

- **What did you choose? What sound do you hear at the beginning of the word? What letter makes that sound?**

- **If you have the matching letter on your bus, put a counter (or marker) on that letter and put the picture beside your bus. If you don't have the letter for the sound, put the picture back in the center of our group.**

- Repeat the process with the next student.

- Continue playing until all bus spaces are covered.

- If you have time, have the students trade buses and play the game again.

Variation: To challenge students, put the cards in a pile face down. Have the first student draw the top card; if she/he cannot use the card, put the card in a discard pile. Continue playing as long as time permits or until all bus spaces are covered.

Bus Lotto Cards

Bus Lotto Cards *(cont.)*

Bus Lotto Cards *(cont.)*

Initial Sounds Matching

Objective: Matching objects to letters

Rationale: Awareness of beginning sounds will be reinforced by identifying the initial sound of an object and matching it to a letter.

Materials: Magnet board, magnetic letters, magnetic objects

Preparation: Place the letters in alphabetical order on the magnet board.

Procedure:

- Seat the children around a large magnet board.
- **We're going to match beginning sounds to the letters.**
- Direct a student to choose a magnetic item.
- **What did you choose? What sound do you hear at the beginning of the word? What letter matches that sound?**
- Direct the student to put the item under the matching letter and repeat the process with the next student.
- When all objects have been placed under their letters, take them off and begin again. Encourage students to choose different items.

Note: This activity can be adapted if magnetic objects are not readily available. Add magnets to the back of picture cards, or match objects to letters at a table or on the floor.

Pocket Chart Sounds Match

Objective: Matching pictures to letters

Rationale: Identifying the initial sound of a picture and matching it to a letter will reinforce awareness of beginning sounds.

Materials: Pocket chart, letter cards (pages 26–31), initial sounds picture cards (pages 67–73)

Preparation: None

Procedure:

- Seat the children around a pocket chart. Letter cards should be placed in chart ahead of time. Lay picture cards face up in front of the pocket chart.

- **Today we're going to match beginning sounds to letters.**

- Direct a student to choose a picture card.

- **What did you choose? What sound do you hear at the beginning of the word? What letter matches that sound?**

- Direct the student to put the picture beside the matching letter and repeat the process with the next student.

- When all pictures have been placed beside their letters, take them off and begin again. Encourage students to choose different pictures.

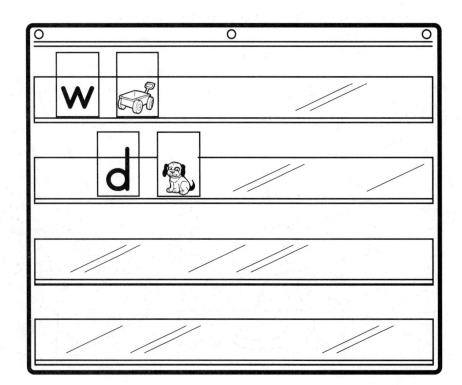

Object/Letter Match

Objective: Matching objects to letters

Rationale: Matching letters and sounds is a crucial pre-reading skill.

Materials: Object tubs for 10–13 letters, a basket

Preparation: An object tub is a bowl or small container with five or six small items all beginning with the same sound. The letter for the sound should be written on the tub or a letter card should be placed beside the tub. You can purchase object tubs or make your own tubs. Put the items from the tubs in the basket.

Procedure:

- Seat the children around a basket of objects.

- **Today we're going to match beginning sounds to letters.**

- Direct a student to choose an object.

- **What did you choose? What sound do you hear at the beginning of the word? What letter matches that sound?**

- **Do you see that letter on one of the tubs? You're right! Put the (name item) in the small tub for the letter (name matching letter).**

- Assist students who are struggling with letters or sounds.

- Repeat the process with the next student.

- When all objects have been placed in the correct tubs, put them back in the basket and begin the activity again.

Picture/Letter Match

Objective: Identifying sounds and letters

Rationale: Naming pictures and letters will reinforce letter and sound recognition.

Materials: A picture card for every letter of the alphabet (pages 67–69), a set of lowercase letters (pages 29–31)

Preparation: None

Procedure:

- Place the picture cards and the letter cards on a table or the floor, face down. Keep the two sets separate (i.e., The picture cards should be together and the letter cards should be together. Do not mix them.)

- Seat the children around the cards. Direct the first child to turn over a picture card.

- **What is the beginning sound for that picture?**

- Have the student make the sound first, then have all students make the beginning sound.

- **Turn over a letter card. What letter is it? Does the letter card match your picture card?**

- If the two cards match, let the student keep the cards. If the cards do not go together, have the student turn both cards face down.

- Let the second child complete each step. Be sure to ask each student to make the beginning sound for the picture and name the letter for each card drawn. Continue around the group until you have used all cards. Repeat the activity if time permits.

Note: This is a variation of Memory or Concentration. Use just $\frac{1}{3}$ of the picture cards and their matching letters the first time you play this game. Use $\frac{1}{2}$ of the picture cards and their matching letters the second time you play the game. After that, add as many cards as your students can successfully use at one time. It is better to play two or three short, successful games with fewer cards than to play one long, frustrating game with all the cards.

Letter/Sound Wheels

Objective: Matching pictures to letters

Rationale: Connecting sounds with the letters that represent them is an important pre-reading skill.

Materials: Letter wheels (pages 118–120), picture pie pieces (pages 77–82)

Preparation: Cut out the letter wheels, leaving each as a whole wheel. Use all of the picture pie pieces from the Initial Sound Wheel game together with the letter wheels for this game.

Procedure:

- Seat the children in a semi circle or at a table. Give each student a wheel. Put the picture pie pieces face down in the center of the group.

- **Today, we're going to name letters and make the sound for each of those letters. We will match beginning sounds to letters.**

- Direct one student to begin by drawing a pie piece.

- **Name the picture that you found. What sound do you hear at the beginning of the word? What letter matches that sound? Is that letter on your wheel?**

- If the pie piece matches any letter on the player's wheel, it should be placed on that letter. If the player cannot use the card, it should be placed face down in the pile.

- Continue around the circle, asking the same questions.

- When every player covers his/her wheel, trade wheels and begin again.

- If you do not have enough time to finish the game, turn over the remaining pie pieces and let the students choose matching cards.

Variation: To make this game easier, lay the picture pie pieces face up.

Letter Sound Wheels

Leave this wheel whole!

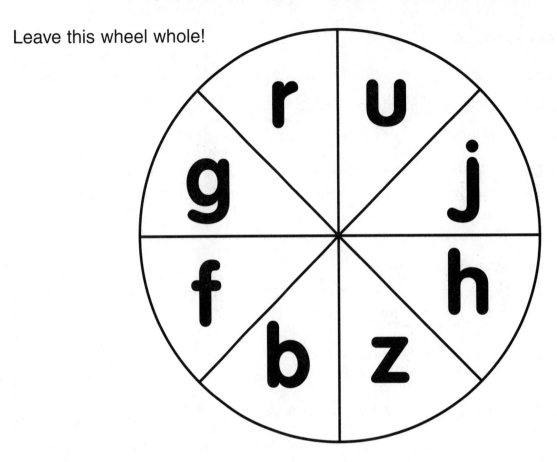

Leave this wheel whole!

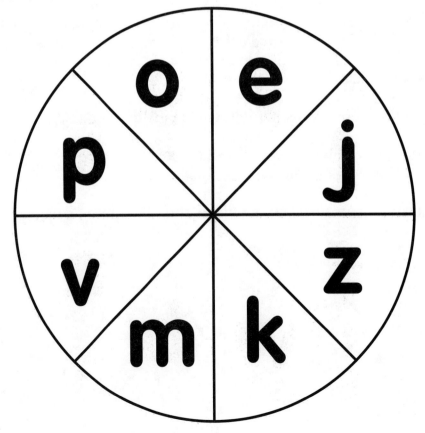

Letter Sound Wheels *(cont.)*

Leave this wheel whole!

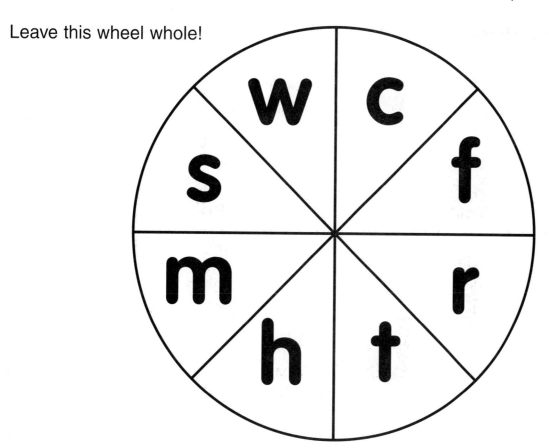

Leave this wheel whole!

Letter Sound Wheels *(cont.)*

Leave this wheel whole!

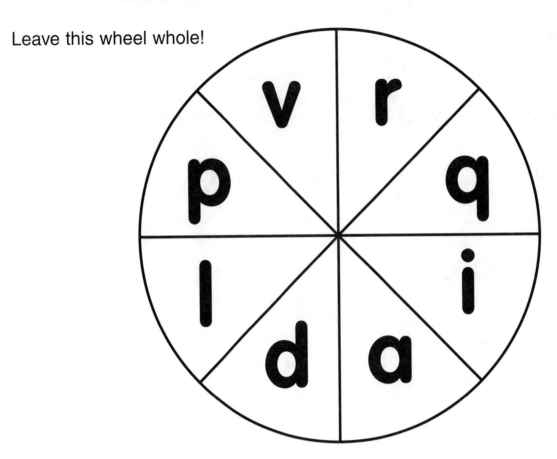

Leave this wheel whole!

Color Word Lotto

Objective: Matching objects to color words

Rationale: Beginning readers need a bank of words that they can read automatically. Color words are meaningful and frequently seen in a classroom setting. Students will become more familiar with the color words through Color Word Lotto.

Materials: A Color Word Lotto card for each player (pages 122–124), small squares (or heart-shaped pieces) of construction paper

Preparation: Copy lotto cards onto white paper or tag. Cut cards apart, but do not color since students need to focus on the color words. Multiple squares of the following colors will also be needed: red, orange, yellow, green, blue, purple, brown, black, pink, gray, white. (Objects may be substituted for the construction squares if you can find enough one-color items.)

Procedure:

• Seat the students around a table. Give each child a lotto card.

• **Today we're going to play Color Word Lotto. You will try to cover each word on your card with a paper square of that color.**

• **(Student's name), draw the top square. What color is it?**

• **If you have the color word (name color) on your card, you may put your square on it. If you don't have the color word, you need to put the square on the discard pile.**

• Continue around the table asking the same questions. Assist, if necessary. When everyone has covered her/his card, trade cards and play again.

Color Word Lotto

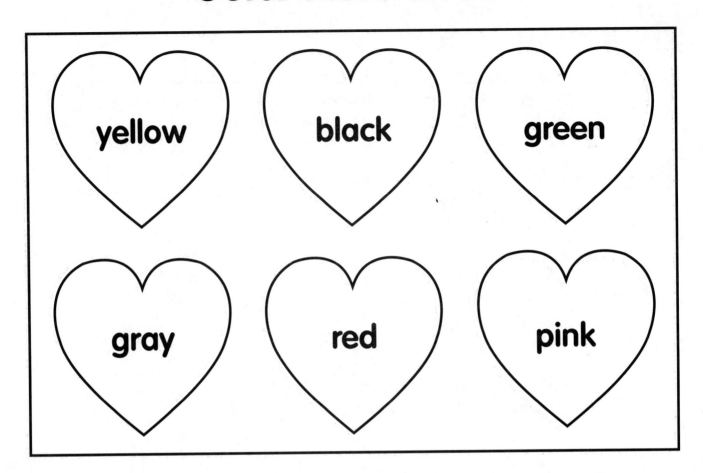

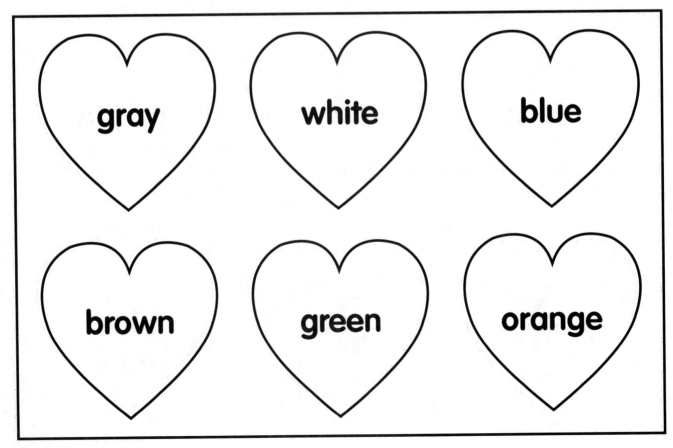

Color Word Lotto *(cont.)*

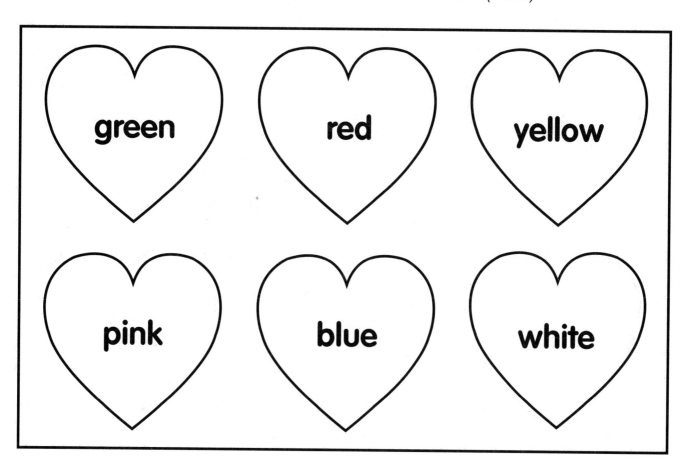

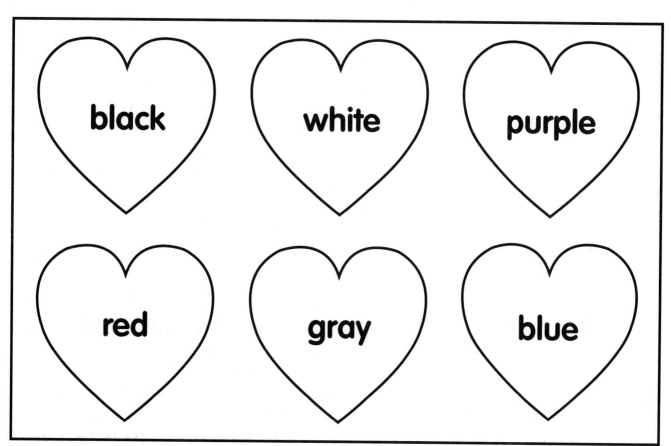

Color Word Lotto *(cont.)*

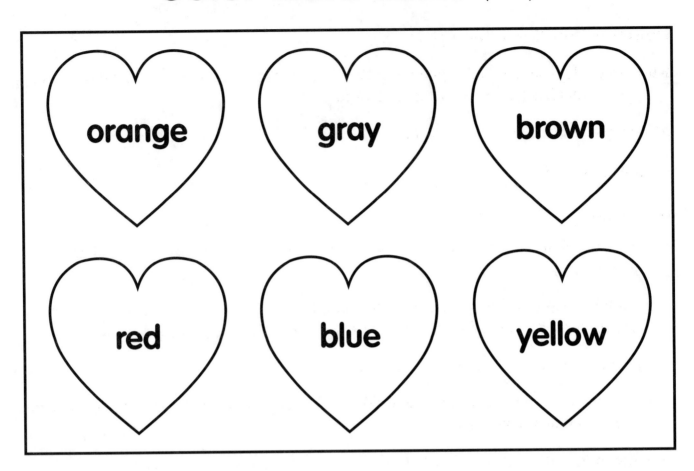

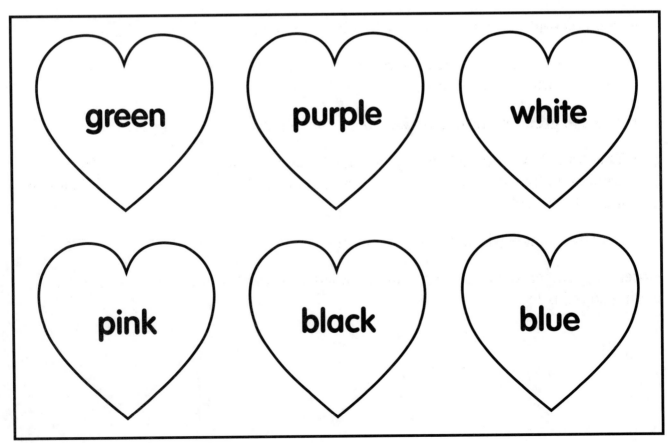

Final Sound Photos

Objective: Isolating the final phoneme

Rationale: This lesson is designed to give students practice isolating the final sound or ending phoneme of familiar words.

Materials: A picture of each student

Preparation: None

Procedure:

- Seat the children at a table. Show the students the cards with pictures of their classmates.

- **Today we are going to play a game using the names of our classmates. I am going to place the cards in a pile, and I will draw the top card.**

- Place cards in a pile in the center of the table.

- (Draw a card) **This is a picture of (Dan). Listen carefully to the last sound of his name. Dan-n-n-n-n-n.**

- Emphasize the last sound or keep making the sound if it is continuant.

- **What sound do you hear? You're right, the last sound in Dan's name is /n/.**

- Continue the game by drawing the cards and saying the names until all of the picture cards have been used.

- **You are great at ending sounds, let's play again!**

- This time, have the student to your right draw a card and say the name. Help emphasize the last sound if those listening have troubling identifying it. Continue around the circle.

- Play the game again until the allotted time is up.

Note: Remember, this is ending sound, not letter. If the student's name is Kathy, the ending sound is /e/, not y.

Cross the River Final Sounds

Objective: Identifying final phonemes

Rationale: The final sound in a word is very difficult to hear. This lesson will provide practice isolating the final sound, using a kinesthetic activity.

Materials: A puppet, a balance beam

Preparation: None

Procedure:

- Seat the children next to a balance beam.

- **Today we are going to play a game called Cross the River. This is (say puppet's name). He is very bossy, and he believes this bridge is his. If you want to cross the river, you have to listen to a word he chooses and tell him its very last sound. When you make the last sound, he will let you cross the river.**

- **Let's practice a few words before we begin.** Practice with these words: tree, hat, car, house, tack, zoo.

- **Let's begin. (Student's name), you may go first. "Who are you?"** The child will then reply, **"It is _____."** **"Okay, then, you may cross my bridge if you can tell me the ending sound of _____ ."**

- Be sure to exaggerate the ending sound, and assist the child if necessary. After the child gives the correct sound, be sure to repeat and reinforce the sound.

- **"Okay, (Student's name), you may cross my bridge."** The child may then walk across the balance beam, and return to the other side, lining up for another turn.

- Suggested Words: ape, bat, bear, bird, bunny, cat, clam, dog, duck, elephant, fish, horse, lamb, kitty, lion, monkey, monster, owl, panda, puppy, rabbit, snail, snake, tiger, turkey, walrus, fox, whale, wolf, apple, bacon, cake, bread, burger, cheese, butter, corn, egg, muffin, spaghetti, toast, watermelon, pizza, pillow, couch, clock, pan, piano, TV, hammer, bone, bicycle, cloud, read, mitt, ring, shoe, watch.

Note: Remember, it is the ending sound, not letter. For example, in the word shoe, the sound is oo, not e.

Final Sound Oddity

Objective: Identifying items with matching final sounds

Rationale: Oddity activities help students focus on similarities and differences. Determining which items belong together will reinforce final sounds.

Materials: A basket of small objects

Preparation: Gather the objects for the basket.

Procedure:

- Seat the children in a semi circle or at a table. Choose two items ending with the same sound and a third item with a different final sound.

- Name each item as you set it on the table or floor.

- **(Student's name), which two items have the same ending sound? What sound do you hear at the end of each word?** If the student has problems, repeat the words, emphasizing the final sound. Allow other students to help, if necessary.

- **Which item is the odd-man out? What sound do you hear at the end of (name object)?** Emphasize final sound if necessary.

- Set the three items aside. Choose three new objects and repeat the process.

- Continue this activity throughout the allotted time. If all objects are used, begin again with different combinations.

Musical Letters

Objective: Recognizing letters of the alphabet

Rationale: Reviewing the alphabet through Musical Letters will enhance letter recognition.

Materials: Large alphabet cards or floor tiles, music

Preparation: If you do not have floor tiles, you can make suitable alphabet cards by cutting 13 sheets of construction paper or tag in half and writing a different letter on each sheet.

Procedure:

- Place the alphabet cards in a circle on the floor or around a large table. Have the students stand around the letters.

- **Today we're going to play Musical Letters. While the music plays, you will walk around the letters. When I stop the music, stop walking.**

- Turn on the music for 5–10 seconds, then turn it off.

- **Put your hand (or your foot) on the letter that is closest to you.**

- **(Student's name), what letter did you land on? Do you know the sound for that letter?**

- If the student does not know the letter, let another student whisper its name. Help with sounds, if necessary. Continue around the circle, giving each student a turn to identify his/her letter and sound.

- **Now turn your letter face down and I will turn the music on. Remember to stop walking when I turn the music off.**

- Repeat the same process. Vary the length of time the music plays. Be sure each student identifies a letter and a sound each time.

- When all letters have been identified, turn them face up so the letters show, then begin again. Challenge students (who are able) to name a word beginning with the letter they are touching. Continue to play as long as time permits.

Medial Sound Game

Objective: Identifying middle sounds

Rationale: Medial sound identification is difficult for most students. This activity provides an opportunity for practice before students begin blending.

Materials: Place markers, a number die, three-sound picture cards (three-sound objects can be substituted), a blank game board

Preparation: Copy and cut out the picture cards from pages 130–134 and laminate, if desired. Use any large, blank game board (or substitute blank individual game boards, page 108).

Procedure:

- Put the game board on a table or the floor. Seat the children around it. Each child should place a game piece on Start. **Listen as I say the word bat slowly. Baaaaaaat. Help me make the aaaaaaaaa sound in the middle of the word bat.**

- **Today, we are going to listen for the sound in the middle of a word as we play a game. (Student's name), you can begin. Shake the die. How many spaces can you move your game piece?**

- **Now, draw a card (or object). Name the picture that you found. What sound do you hear in the middle of (name picture)?** Remember to focus on the sound, not the letter.

- You may have to help the student identify the initial sound and the final sound before she/he can focus on the medial sound. If the student still has trouble, say the word slowly. Emphasize the medial sound. Piiiiiiiig.

- **Great! You heard the iiiiii sound in the middle of pig. You can move your game piece forward one more space.**

- Continue around the group, following the same procedure. If a student cannot hear or identify the middle sound even with help, the game piece should not move forward another space. Offer as much assistance as necessary, however, so all students experience success most of the time.

- If you run out of cards, mix up the cards in the discard pile. Continue playing until all players reach Finish. Begin the game again if time permits.

3-Sound Picture Cards

witch

moose

ant

toad

seal

heart

note

pop

tug

3-Sound Picture Cards (cont.)

fly

mouse

tub

barn

mat

coat

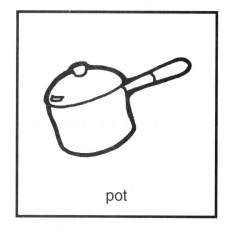

pot

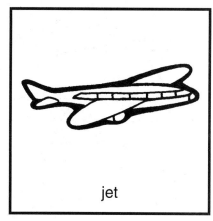

jet

house

girl

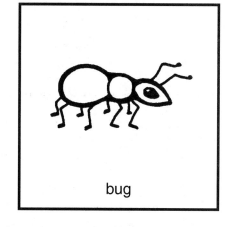

bug

boat

3-Sound Picture Cards *(cont.)*

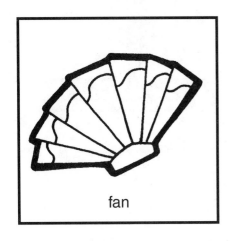
fan

sun

hen

sheep

goat

doll

cub

goose

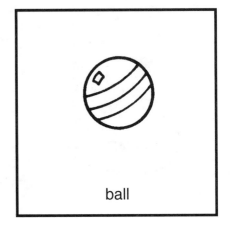
ball

cup

bat

mice

3-Sound Picture Cards *(cont.)*

ham

log

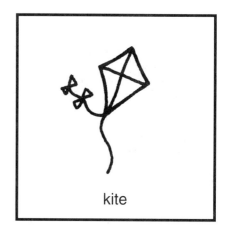

kite

man

chin

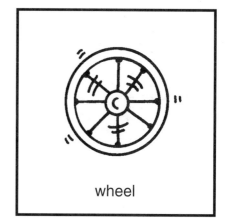

wheel

cat

pig

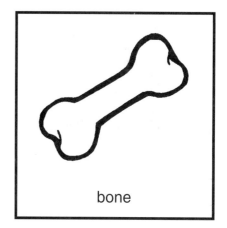

bone

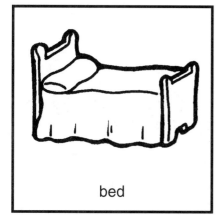

bed

rat

rose

3-Sound Picture Cards *(cont.)*

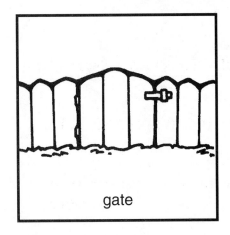

gate

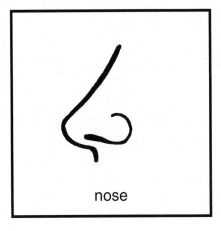

nose

soap

hat

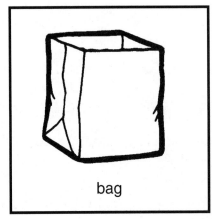

bag

dog

cake

duck

tree

mop

light

moon

Mirrors and Medial Sounds

Objective: Identifying the middle sound

Rationale: Students will practice isolating the medial sound in consonant, vowel, consonant words.

Materials: Three sound cards, picture cards of three-sound words (pages 130–134), mirror for each child, easel, rubber band

Preparation: To make sound cards, glue a red piece of construction paper to a blue piece of construction paper. Cut into fourths and laminate. Use three pieces for this activity.

Procedure:

- Seat the students in a semi circle on the carpet.

- **Today we are going to practice naming the middle sound in three sound words.**

- **We will begin by drawing a picture card. (Student's name), will you draw the first card and tell us what it is?**

- **Great, it is a (cat). We have already practiced beginning and ending sounds of words, so they should be easy for us.**

- **Today, we are going to listen for the middle sound.**

- **I will put up three sound cards, because our picture card has three sounds.**

- Place the three sound cards with the blue sides showing on an easel tray. When students give the beginning, middle, and ending sounds of the word, turn those cards to red.

- **(Cat), the word is (cat). Who can tell me the beginning sound?** (Turn the first card to red as the students identify the sound.)

- **(Cat), the word is (cat). Who can tell me the ending sound?** (Turn the last card to red as the students identify the sound.)

Mirrors and Medial Sounds *(cont.)*

- **Now, we have only one card left to turn over. It is the middle sound. This is usually a very hard sound to hear, and it will take us some practice to become good at hearing it.**

- **Let's say the word very slowly, just as if we were pulling it with a rubber band.**

- Show the students a rubber band and stretch it out slowly as you model the word.

- **/C/.../a/.../t/, cat.**

- **I am going to give everyone a mirror.** (Pass out mirrors.) **Now we are going to say our word as a rubber band. /C/.../a/.../t/, cat.**

- **This time, I want you to look in a mirror as we are saying the word as a rubber band, and I will say stop when we reach the middle sound.**

- **/c/.../a/... STOP! Everyone, look at the shape of your mouth. Can you see your mouth open and your tongue on your bottom teeth? That is the sound /a/. It is found in the middle of the word (cat).**

- **Look in the mirror as we say /a/ together. /a/.........(hold out the sound.)**

- **Now, who can tell me the middle sound in cat?**

- **Great, it is /a/! Now we are ready to turn over the middle sound box to its red side.**

- **Okay, let's try this again with another picture card.**

- Turn the sound boxes back to blue and begin again.

- Continue playing the game. Follow the above script for the rest of the cards in the pile.

Alphabet Bear Slide

Objective: Vocalizing sounds of letters

Rationale: Identifying the initial sound of letters with movement will reinforce the sounds of letters.

Materials: Alphabet bears (pages 14–16), picture of a slide for each child (page 138), basket (optional)

Preparation: Copy and laminate a slide for each student.

Procedure:

- Seat the children around a table.

- **Today we're going to practice the sounds of letters.**

- **We are going to pretend that the bears in this basket are going to the playground. Each bear would like a turn to go down the slide.**

- **(Student's name), you go first. Choose a bear out of the basket and place him at the top of the slide. Now, tell us the name of his letter.**

- **You're right! The letter on the bear is (A). What sound does your (A) bear make?**

- **Now it is time for him to go down the slide. As he does, he will be so excited, he will squeal his sound all the way down. /A..a..a..a..a..a/.**

- Continue play around the table as time allows.

Alphabet Bear Slide

Blending Two-Sound Words

Objective: Blending two sound words

Rationale: Children need to understand that all words are composed of strings of phonemes. This lesson will allow the students to manipulate the phonemes.

Materials: Two blocks for each child

Preparation: If blocks are not available, use bingo disks, cardboard squares, checkers, or whatever else is handy.

Procedure:

- Seat the students around a table.

- **Today we are going to practice listening to words that have two sounds.**

- **Listen to my first word. It is *my*. Demonstrate the word by saying the sounds slowly, /m/…/i/… .**

- **Repeat the word with me, *my*! Now say it with me slowly, /m/…/i/….**

- Now take the two blocks and place them in front of you.

- **Listen to the word my as I push the blocks, one for each sound. /M/…/i… .**

- Push the blocks forward one at a time as you say the sounds, /m/…/i/….

- Each block represents a sound, so make sure that you push the block as you say the sound.

- **Okay, I am going to give each of you two blocks, and we are going to try some two sound words together.**

- Give children two blocks apiece and have them lay the blocks in a horizontal row in front of them.

- Try the word *my*, with the children moving their blocks as you move yours. Remember to say the sound as you move the block.

Blending Two-Sound Words *(cont.)*

- **The next word we are going to try is /m/…../e/…Who can say this word fast?**

- **Great, let's say the word me slowly together. /m/…/e/… .**

- **Now let's move a block for each sound as we say the word slowly.**

- **/M/…/e/… .**

- **What word do the sounds, /m/…/e/… . make?**

- Remember to always return the sounds back to the word.

- Continue the activity with the following two sound words. Each time, remember to say the word slowly to the children at first.

my	is	as	an
no	am	by	bow
add	all	it	shoe
up	buy	ray	at
bay	so	off	zoo
me	on	day	car
how			

Note: Remember to stay with two-sound words for this activity.

Blending Three-Sound Words

Objective: Extending phoneme analysis and synthesis to consonant-vowel-consonant words

Rationale: Children need to understand that all words are composed of strings of phonemes. This lesson will allow the students to manipulate the phonemes.

Materials: Three blocks for each child

Preparation: If blocks are not available, use bingo disks, cardboard squares, checkers, or whatever else is handy.

Procedure:

- Seat the students around a table.

- **Today we are going to practice listening to words that have three sounds.**

- **Listen to my first word. It is *rice*. Demonstrate the word by saying the sounds slowly, /r/……../i/………/s/.**

- **Repeat the word with me, *rice*! Now say it with me slowly, /r……../i/………/s/.**

- Now take the three blocks and place them in front of you.

- **Children, listen to the word rice as I push the blocks, one for each sound, /r/…….. /i/………/s/.**

- Push the blocks forward one at a time as you say the sounds, /r/……../i/………/s/.

- Each block represents a sound, so make sure that you push the block as you say the sound.

- **Okay, I am going to give each of you three blocks, and we are going to try some three sound words together.**

- Give children three blocks and have them lay the blocks in a horizontal row in front of them.

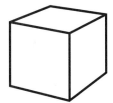 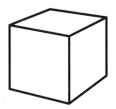 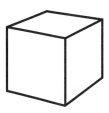

Blending Three-Sound Words *(cont.)*

- Try the word *rice*, with the children moving their blocks as you move yours. Remember to say the sound as you move the block.

- **The next word we are going to try is /s/.../a/.../l/. Who can say this word fast for me?**

- **Great, let's say the word *sail* slowly together. /S/.../a/.../l/.**

- **Now let's move a block for each sound as we say the word slowly.**

- **/S/.../a/.../l/.**

- **What word do the sounds, /s/.../a/.../l/ make?**

- Remember to always return the sounds back to the word.

- Continue the activity with the following three sound words. Each time, remember at first to say the word slowly to the children.

name	**mad**	**make**	**pup**
meat	**Bill**	**roar**	**sour**
bone	**same**	**seal**	**chin**
tad	**moon**	**bite**	**cup**
hedge	**cat**	**ban**	**bone**
wake	**cheese**	**deal**	**witch**
soap	**ham**	**bit**	**toad**
love	**ran**	**mash**	**moose**
mice	**wheel**	**nose**	**beef**
gate	**kite**	**note**	**tug**

Giant Blending

Objective: Synthesizing words from their separate phonemes

Rationale: Children need to understand that all words are composed of strings of phonemes. This lesson will treat words phoneme by phoneme.

Materials: Picture cards of three sound words (pages 130–134)

Preparation: None

Procedure:

- Seat the students in a circle.

- Tell the following tale:

    Once upon a time, there was a friendly giant who loved to give people presents. The giant wanted to tell what the present was before giving it away! The problem was he had a very strange way of talking. If he was going to tell a child his present was a bike, he would say "/b/ - /i/ - /k/."

- **When the child guessed the present, the giant would be happy!**

- **Now, I will pretend to be the giant. I will name a surprise for one of you. When you figure out what the surprise is, I will show you a picture of it.**

- Draw a card and pronounce the name of the present, phoneme by phoneme. Turn to the child on your right. **What is the name of the present?**

- When the child guesses the word, give her/him the card. Draw another card and pronounce the name of the new present, phoneme by phoneme. Call on the next child in the circle. Hand the child the card when he/she names the present.

- Continue playing the game for the allotted time, giving students assistance as needed.

Mother May I? Blending

Objective: Blending phonemes

Rationale: Children need to understand that all words are composed of strings of phonemes. This lesson will treat words phoneme by phoneme as the students practice their blending and segmenting skills.

Materials: Blending/Segmenting Word List (page 145)

Preparation: None

Procedure:

- This game is a version of Mother May I? which is played with the children standing in a line on one side of the room, while the Mother stands on the other side. The Mother calls on one child and gives a direction. Before following the direction, the child must ask, "Mother May I?" If he/she forgets to ask for permission, the child must return to his/her spot. The Mother continues giving directions to each child in turn until one child reaches her; the first child to reach Mother is the winner.

- **Today we are going to play a game called Mother May I. You are going to stand there, and I will be Mother. The object of the game is to be the first one to reach Mother.**

- **When it is your turn, you will move ahead the number of steps to equal the sounds in a word that I say. For example, if I say /c/.../a/.../t/, you will tell me the word is cat. Then, you may move ahead 3 spaces, one step for each sound.**

- Model this as you move forward, one step for each sound.

- **Now, let's begin. (Student's name), let's start with you. Listen to these sounds. _____ _____ _____. (Student's name), what is my word?**

- **You're right, the word is _____. You may move ahead _____ spaces as you make the sounds for the word _____. As you say the sounds of the word, you may move one footstep with each sound you hear.**

- Play the game several times. Make sure the students are blending and segmenting accurately. Assist as much as necessary.

Blending/Segmenting Word List

Use this word list when two-, three-, and four-sound words are needed for the following activities:

- **Mother May I? Blending**
- **Blending/Segmenting Game**
- **Other Similar Activities**

rat	log	sat	put	cup	zoo
neck	hate	love	dance	party	door
hat	from	house	let	pig	bat
girl	boy	desk	tub	jug	ran
cheese	shoe	dart	sack	bug	from
man	fly	tree	pie	key	car
doll	soap	nose	bag	hose	mop
king	rock	ant	moon	top	boat
fan	bee	ball	sun	frog	sled
fox	spoon	truck	bread	flag	box
clock	mouse	clown	house	crown	tick

Duck, Duck Goose Segmenting

cat	dog	duck	goat	lamb	cub
calf	sheep	hen	goose	cow	horse
puppy	pony	bunny	kitten	turkey	snake

Blending and Segmenting Game

Objective: Blending phonemes to make words

Rationale: Blending is an important pre-reading skill. Students will have an opportunity to practice blending as they have fun playing a game.

Materials: Game pieces, number die, a game board with blank spaces, Blending/Segmenting Word List (page 145)

Preparation: Use any large, blank game board or substitute individual game boards by copying page 108.

Procedure:

- Seat the children around the game board. **Today we're going to play a game. We will be blending words. Each time you figure out a word, you will move your game piece an extra space on the board.**

- **(Student's name), you will be first. Shake the number die and move that many spaces. Listen as I sound out a word. Tell me the word when you know it. /C…a…t/. What word can you make from the sounds /c…a…t/?**

- If the student cannot identify the word, ask the other students to help. (They should not help until this time.)

- **You're right! I was making the sounds for the word cat. Move your game piece one more space on the board. Let's all make the sounds for cat together. /C…a…t/, cat.**

- Turn to the next child. **(Student's name), you will be next. Shake the number die and move that many spaces. Listen as I sound out a word. Tell me the word when you know it. /D…o…g/. What word can you make from the sounds /d…o…g/?**

- Offer as much assistance as necessary since the emphasis of this activity is on blending and segmenting, not winning!

- **Let's all sound out dog together. /D…o…g/, dog.** Continue around the group, segmenting words from the Blending/Segmenting Word List.

I Can Spell Game

Objective: Spelling words with letters

Rationale: The ultimate purpose of phonemic awareness is to guide students to the reading of words, using letters. This activity will provide an opportunity to practice matching letters on a game mat in order to spell words.

Materials: An I Can Spell game card for each player (pages 148–150), a grab bag (a box or a bowl can be substituted), a set of tactile or magnetic letters, a spinner or a number die

Preparation: Copy and cut apart the I Can Spell game boards.

Procedure:

- Seat the students around a table, giving each a game card.
- **Today we're going to spell words. (Students name), you twirl the spinner first (or shake the die).**
- **Now take that many letters out of the grab bag and see if the words on your game board have any of the letters that you drew. If you have some that don't match, simply put them back in the bag.**
- As a word is completed, assist the student in reading it.
- Continue around the table until all words are spelled. Trade cards and play again, if time permits.

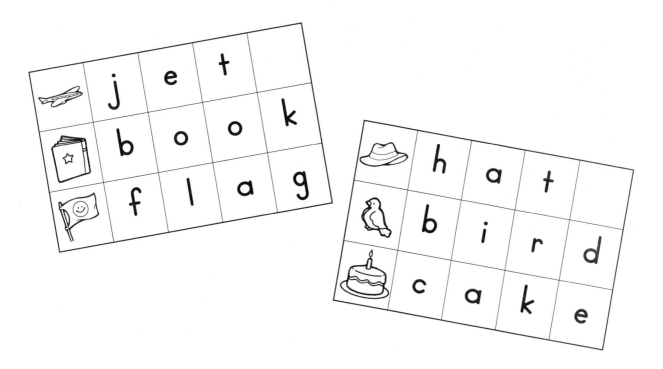

I Can Spell Game Cards

✈	j	e	t	
📖	b	o	o	k
🚩	f	l	a	g

🎩	h	a	t	
🐦	b	i	r	d
🎂	c	a	k	e

I Can Spell Game Cards *(cont.)*

	c	a	t	
	l	a	m	b
	f	r	o	g

	l	i	o	n
	n	a	i	l
	k	i	n	g

I Can Spell Game Cards *(cont.)*

	n	o	s	e
	k	i	t	e
	n	e	s	t

	f	i	s	h
	s	u	n	
	t	r	e	e

Alphabet Lotto

Objective: Matching objects to letters

Rationale: It is important to frequently review the alphabet. The game will reinforce letter recognition as students practice connecting letters to sounds.

Materials: An Alphabet Lotto card for each player (pages 152–154), objects to match the corresponding letters

Preparation: Choose objects from your object tubs for this game; some sounds need two items because the letter is listed twice. Copy, laminate (if desired) and cut apart the lotto cards.

Procedure:

- Seat the students around a table. Give each child a lotto card.

- **Today we're going to play Alphabet Lotto. You will try to cover each letter on your card with something that starts with the letter's sound.**

- **(Student's name), draw one item out of the basket. What is it? What sound do you hear at the beginning of the word? What letter makes that sound?**

- **If you have the letter _____ on your card, you may put the (name object) on it. If you don't have the letter _____, you need to put the object back in the basket.**

- Continue around the table asking the same questions. Be sure each student identifies not only the item and its beginning sound, but also the letter that makes that sound. Assist, if necessary.

- When everyone has covered her/his card, put objects back in the basket and trade cards. Continue to play for the allotted time.

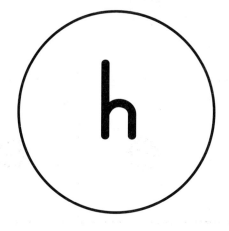 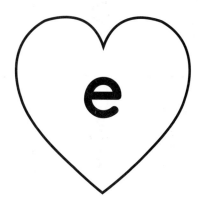

Alphabet Lotto

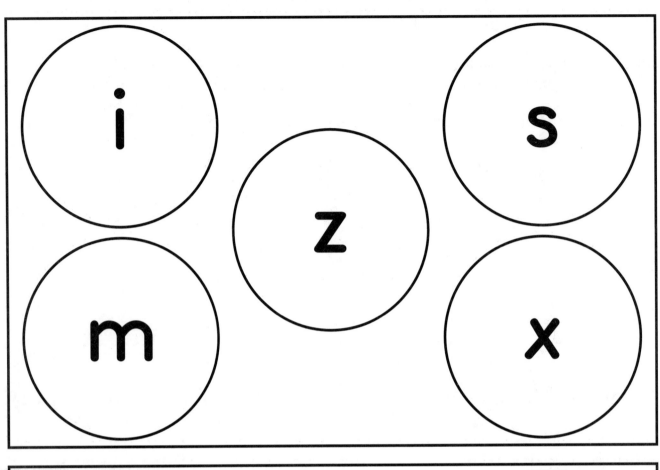

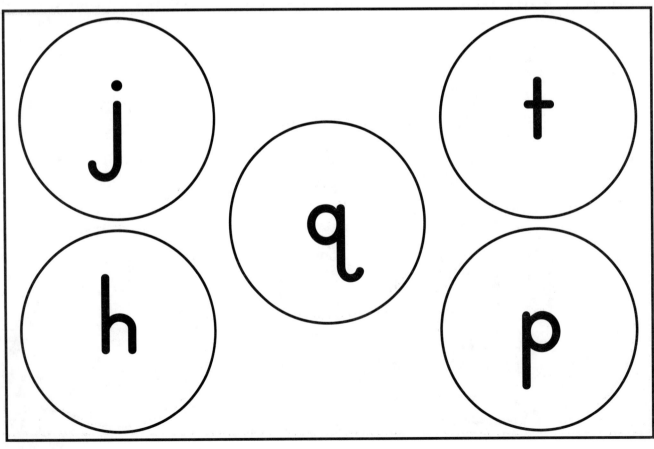

Alphabet Lotto *(cont.)*

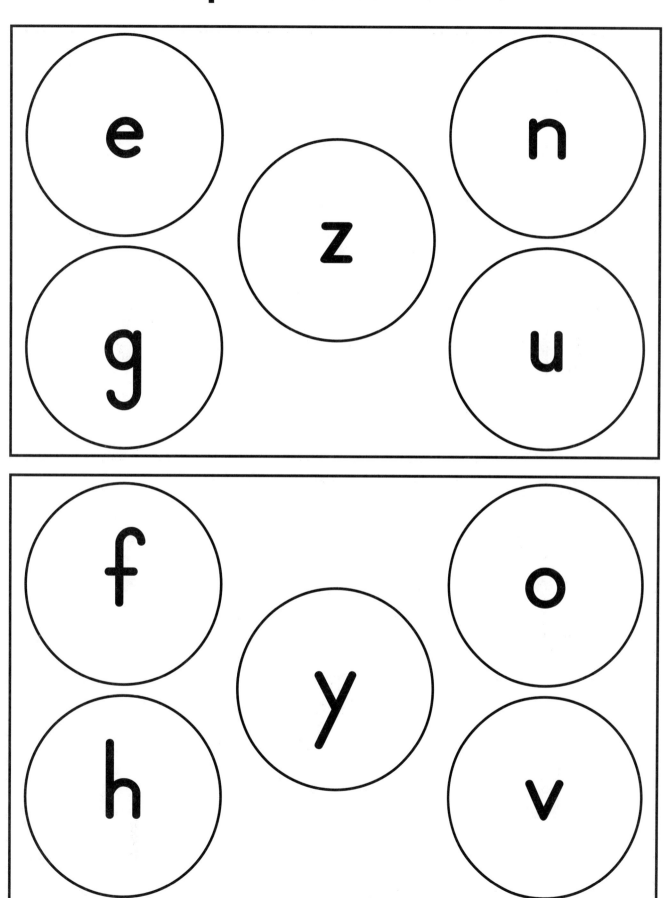

Alphabet Lotto *(cont.)*

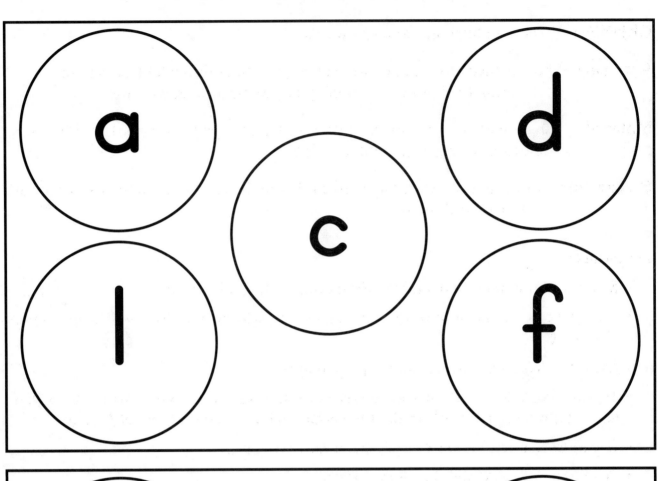

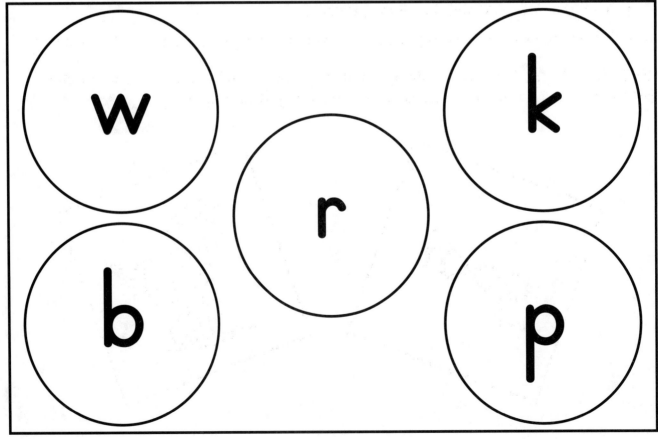

Animal Lotto Blending

Objective: Blending phonemes to make words

Rationale: Students need to focus on individual phonemes through blending and segmenting to continue developing phonemic awareness skills.

Materials: Bingo markers, an Animal Lotto card for each player (pages 157–159), a word card for each animal (page 156)

Preparation: Copy and cut apart the word cards and the Animal Lotto cards. Color and laminate, if desired.

Procedure:

- Seat the children around a table. Give each student a lotto card.
- **Today we're going to play Animal Lotto. We will be blending words as we play the game.**
- Draw the word card for cat and say its sounds.
- **If you have a /c/ /a/ /t/ on your page, put a marker on it. What word did I just say? That's right! Let's make the sounds for cat together, /c/ /a/ /t/, cat.**
- **If you have a cat on your page, put a marker on it.**
- Draw the next card and repeat the procedure.
- Continue until you have segmented all words. Change lotto cards and play again.

Variation: At another time, challenge students (who are able) to be the teacher and segment the animal names. Assist with segmenting, if necessary.

Animal Lotto Word Cards

pig	cow	turkey
duck	horse	sheep
hen	goat	rooster
dog	goose	cat

Animal Lotto Cards

Animal Lotto Cards *(cont.)*

Animal Lotto Cards *(cont.)*

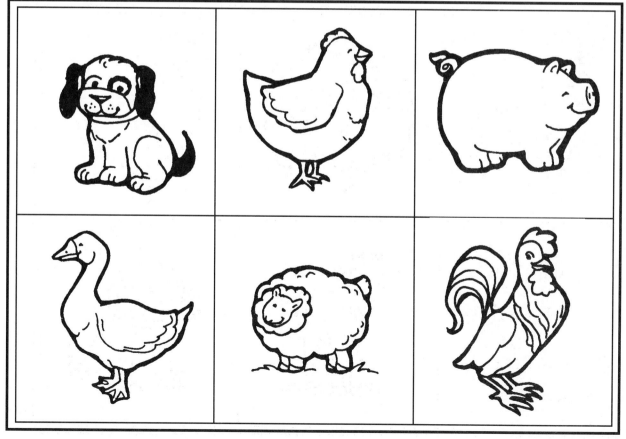

Musical Blending and Segmenting

Objective: Segmenting phonemes

Rationale: Blending and segmenting activities help students focus on individual phonemes.

Materials: Music, three-sound picture cards (pages 130–134)

Preparation: Choose 12–20 three-sound pictures and enlarge them with a copy machine (or substitute smaller pictures).

Procedure:

- Place the cards in a circle on the floor or around a large table. Seat the children around the cards.

- **Today we're going to play a game. We will be segmenting and blending words. Listen to these sounds…. /d/ /o/ /g/. What word did I just say? That's right! Let's say the sounds for dog together, /d/ /o/ /g/, dog. Who can point to the picture of the dog in our circle?**

- Continue until you have segmented all picture cards; skip around the circle, however, so you aren't doing the cards in order.

- **Now, let's play the game. You will walk around the cards as the music plays. When the music stops, you stop! Each of you will have a turn to make the sounds for the picture that is right beside you.**

- Turn the music on for a few seconds. Stop the music.

- **Who wants to be first? What are the sounds for your picture?**

- Go around the circle with each student attempting to segment one picture card. Assist as much as necessary.

- When all students have segmented a picture card, turn the music on and walk around the circle again. After a few seconds, stop the music and repeat the segmenting process.

- Continue playing for the allotted time.

Play Dough Words

Objective: Naming letters and making words

Rationale: Students need to use the letters of the alphabet in words to gain an understanding of their importance.

Materials: Play dough, play dough word cards (pages 162–165)

Preparation: Color, cut apart, and laminate the word cards. Make additional word cards, with or without pictures, if desired.

Procedure:

- Seat the children at a table. Give each child a word card.

- **Today we're going to name letters and make words. We will make the letters from play dough.**

- Demonstrate how to roll the play dough into a snake and form a letter on a word card. Assist students, if necessary.

- **Name the letters on your card. What word do your letters spell?**

- Help the students blend the words that can be sounded out letter-by-letter (hat, sun).

- As a child completes a word, trade cards. Continue until he/she has completed all word cards or the time is up.

Note: Purchase play dough or try this fun recipe.

   3 cups flour

   $\frac{1}{2}$ cup salt

   3 packages unsweetened drink mix

   3 tablespoons cooking oil

   2 cups water (may be a little more or less)

Mix flour, salt, and drink mix together. Add oil. Add one cup of water. Knead, adding more water as needed. Store in an airtight container.

Play Dough Word Cards

Play Dough Word Cards *(cont.)*

Play Dough Word Cards *(cont.)*

Play Dough Word Cards *(cont.)*

flower

worm

bug

Duck, Duck, Goose Segmenting

Objective: Segmenting words

Rationale: Segmenting will be reinforced through a game.

Materials: Blending/Segmenting Word List (page 145)

Preparation: None

Procedure:

- A large area will be needed for this game. Have students sit in a circle.

- **Today we're going to play a game. We will be sounding out words. Listen to this word...pig. What sounds do you hear? We're going to use the sounds of words to play a game like Duck, Duck, Goose.**

- **(Student's name), you will be first. Walk around the outside of the circle. As you say each sound of the word pig, touch someone's head. When you say the whole word, run around the circle.**

- **Let's try it. /P/ /i/ /g/.../p/ /i/ /g/...pig. Now run around the circle! (Name of student tapped), you stand up and chase (first student's name).**

- It the tapped student catches the first student, do not have him/her sit in the middle of the circle. Just continue with the game so no one misses the opportunity to segment.

- **(Name of tapped student), it's your turn to say the sound now. What sounds do you hear in chick? That's right.... /ch/ /i/ /k/. Walk around the circle as you say the sounds. When you say the word, run!**

- Make sure kids are making good choices so everyone has an equal amount of turns.

- Assist with segmenting as much as necessary. Continue as time permits.

- Most words that you choose for the students to segment should have two, three or four sounds. You can choose any word, but the students especially enjoy playing this game using animal names. See the Blending/Segmenting Word List for suggestions.

Sight Word Game

Objective: Building a sight word vocabulary

Rationale: Children need a good sight word vocabulary to be successful readers.

Materials: Sight word cards (pages 168–170), a big pot (or container)

Preparation: Copy and cut apart the sight word cards. Laminate if desired.

Procedure:

- Seat the students around a table.

- **Today we are going to play a game using some of our sight words.**

- **You will take turns drawing a card out of the pot and capturing it for your own.**

- **Okay, (student's name), you draw first. We will sing this song as you draw.**

- **(Susie), (Susie), will you read this word for me? (Sing to the tune of It's raining, it's pouring).**

- Allow the students to take turns drawing words.

- If a student does not know the word, another student can capture it from him.

- When the cards have all been played, dump them back into the pot, and begin again.

- Make additional word cards if you would like to extend this lesson. Use the following list or any sight word collection for suggestions.

a	of	he	was
for	as	his	or
had	by	that	with
they	this	have	from

Sight Words

I

see

the

like

you

me

up

in

Sight Words *(cont.)*

and	at
are	is
on	it
can	did

Sight Words *(cont.)*

my	to
said	go
do	no
yes	am

Blending with Letters

Objective: Identifying letters and sounding out words

Rationale: Connecting letters and sounds together and blending them into words will help students continue the reading process.

Materials: Letter magnets or letter cards (pages 29–31), magnet board or pocket chart

Preparation: None

Procedure:

- Seat the students in front of a magnet board (or pocket chart if you are using letter cards).

- **Today we're going to make words. (Student's name), find the letter *c* and put it on the magnet board (or in the pocket chart). What sound does *c* make?**

- Turn to the next student. **Put the letter *a* beside the *c*. What sound does *a* make?**

- With each new letter, turn to the next student.

- **Put the letter *t* beside the *a*. What sound does *t* make?**

- **Let's blend those three sounds together. /C…a…t/. What word did we just sound out? You're right, the word is cat! Let's sound it out again; pay close attention to the letters.**

- **/C…a…t/, cat.**

- Point to each letter as you make its sound.

- **Let's try another word. Take away the *c* and put up the letter *b*. What sound does *b* make? What is the second sound? What is the third sound? Let's put the three sounds together.**

- **/B…a…t/. What is that word? Let's sound it out again.**

- Blend the letter sounds together slowly as you point to each letter, then say the word normally.

/B…a…t/

Blending with Letters *(cont.)*

- Repeat the same process for the words *hat*, *sat*, *mat*, and *rat*.

- **Let's try a new set of rhyming words. We'll need to take down all of the letters this time.**

- **Find the letter *p* and put it on the magnet board. What sound does it make? Put the letter *i* beside the *p*. What sound does it make? Put the letter *g* beside the *i*. What sound does it make?**

- **Let's sound the whole word out now. /P…i…g/. What is the word? Let's sound it out again, /p…i…g/, pig.**

- Point to each letter as you make its sound.

- Repeat the process, changing the word to *big* and then to *fig*.

- Have students change all letters and sound out a new word (i.e., dog, cup, or red). Change the beginning letter to make a rhyming word to sound out.

- Continue as time permits.

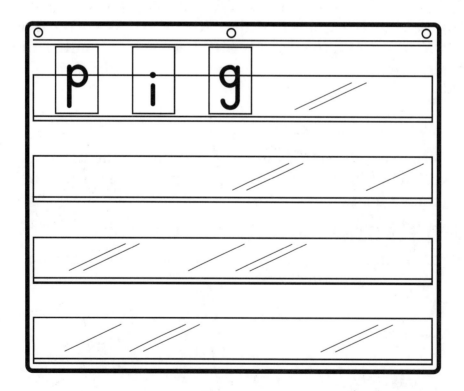

Sight Word Bingo

Objective: Building a sight word vocabulary

Rationale: Children need a good sight word vocabulary to be successful readers.

Materials: Sight word cards (pages 168–170), Sight Word Bingo mats (pages 174–176), Bingo markers

Preparation: Copy and cut apart the Bingo mats. Laminate, if desired.

Procedure:

- Seat the students around a table, and give each student a Bingo mat.

- **Today we are going to play Bingo using our sight word cards.**

- **When I call out a word, check your card to see if you have a match. If you do, place a Bingo marker on that space.**

- Say the word first, and allow the students a few seconds to find the word, then show the card to help find the match.

- **When you have covered an entire card, yell Bingo! Then we will check to see if you are the winner.**

- When checking the card, have the winner read (with your help), the words he/she has covered on the card. Then, play again!

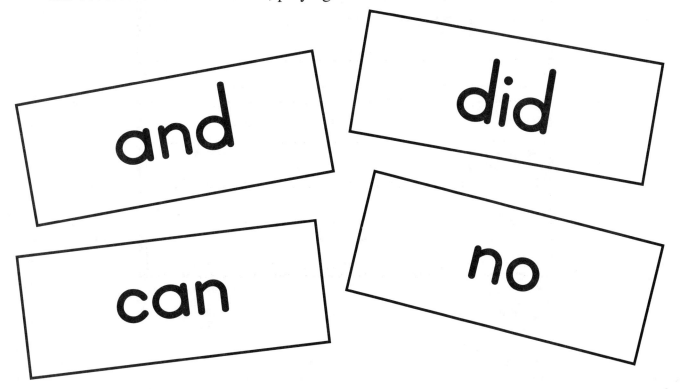

Sight Word Bingo Mats

do	yes
am	is
on	it

and	no
can	am
are	did

Sight Word Bingo Mats *(cont.)*

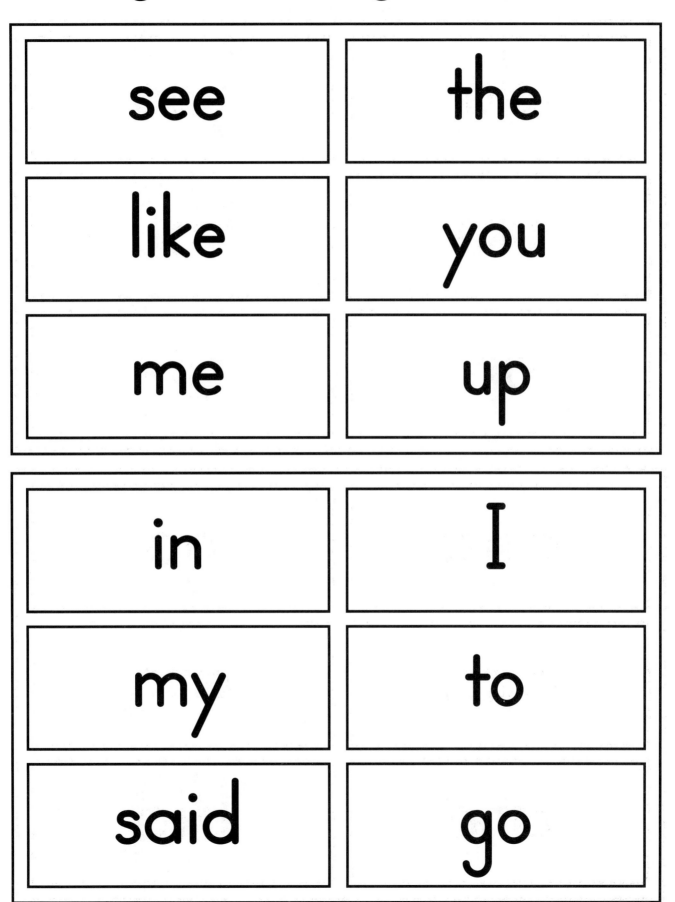

see	the
like	you
me	up

in	I
my	to
said	go

Sight Word Bingo Mats *(cont.)*

are	is
do	you
up	me

you	go
no	can
said	like

Word Counting Game

Objective: Counting the number of words in a sentence

Rationale: Beginning readers need an awareness of print. They need to be able to identify words separately and within a sentence.

Materials: A blank game board, game pieces or markers, sentence strips (pages 178–183)

Preparation: Copy the sentence strips on tag. Cut between each strip to make sentence strips; keep all strips the same length so students cannot identify letters, words, or sentences by the size of the strip. Make additional sentence strips to fit your class if desired. Make one copy of the game board (page 108) for each player, or substitute one large, blank game board.

Procedure:

- Seat the students at a table or on the floor. Give each student a game board. If you are using one game board, place it in the middle. The tag strips should be in the center of the group.

- Have each student choose a game piece and put it on Start.

- **Today we're going to play a word game. (Student's name), you will be first.**

- **Draw a strip. Does your strip have a letter, a word, or a sentence on it?**

- Let the other students assist, if necessary.

- If the student draws a letter, let him/her move forward one space. If the student draws a word, let him/her move forward two spaces. If the student draws a sentence, have him/her count the number of words in the sentence and move forward that number of spaces.

- **That's right, (student's name)! You drew a sentence. How many words do you see in your sentence? Count them. Since your sentence has _____ words, you can move forward _____ spaces.**

- Continue around the group in this fashion. If you finish the game, mix up the strips and begin again. Play until the allotted time is up.

Sentence Strips

I want to go!

cat

a

The cat is fat.

you

h

is

I like to play.

stop

p

You are my friend.

go

f

to

The pig is silly.

she

q

The horse is big.

dad

v

mom

We saw the jet!
of
m
He can run fast.
and
t
up

I am happy!
on
s
Is the cat black?
was
k
are

What time is it?
the
b
The game is fun.
can
o
like

Alphabet Mix-up

Objective: Recognizing the alphabet in mixed form

Rationale: The alphabet is encountered in an intermixed fashion in "real" reading situations. This activity will give students practice in visual discrimination of the alphabet in mixed form.

Materials: A poster of mixed alphabet letters, highlighting tape

Preparation: Choose a poster size large enough for your group. Write all 52 letters on the poster, mixing capital and lowercase letters randomly. Highlighting tape can be purchased from teacher supply stores or catalogs as well as from some office supply stores. It is a self-sticking, removable, colored tape that temporarily lets you highlight words, letters, or sentences. It can be removed without damaging your instructional materials.

Procedure:

- Seat the children in a semi circle.

- **Today we are going to play an alphabet game. I have made a large poster that has upper-and lowercase alphabet letters mixed throughout it.**

- **Before we begin the game, let's say the letters together as I point to them.**

- Have the students read the letters as you point, tracking left to right, top to bottom.

- **Now, let's begin the game. I will go first.**

- **I am thinking of the letter, capital N. (Student's name), will you put this piece of tape on top of the letter, capital N?**

- **Okay, (Student's name), now it is your turn. What letter are you thinking of?**

- Going around the semi circle, have the next student mask the letter.

- Continue playing the game, until all the letters are masked, or the allotted time is up.

- If time allows, have the students take turns using the pointer and tracking the letters while others say them.

Sight Word Fishing

Objective: Building a sight word vocabulary

Rationale: Children need a good sight word vocabulary to build an automatism towards becoming successful readers.

Materials: Sight word fish cards (Pages 186–190), paper clips, a fishing rod, a magnet, a small curtain (optional)

Preparation: Laminate and cut out the sight word fish cards and attach a paper clip to each one. Attach a magnet to the end of the fishing pole line. Set up a curtain and place the fish on the other side.

Procedure:

- Seat the students on the floor.

- **Today we are going to fish for sight words.**

- **We are going to take turns fishing over the curtain for a sight word.**

- **Okay, (student's name), you go fishing first. Throw the fishing pole over the curtain (or into a pond). (Student's name), you go behind the curtain and choose a word to attach to his pole.**

- **Now, reel in your sight word. What is the word?**

- If the student can read the word, he may keep his catch. If he cannot read the word, he must throw the fish back into the pond.

- Continue play as time allows.

Sight Word Fish

Sight Word Fish *(cont.)*

Sight Word Fish (cont.)

did

are

mom

dad

stop

we

Sight Word Fish *(cont.)*

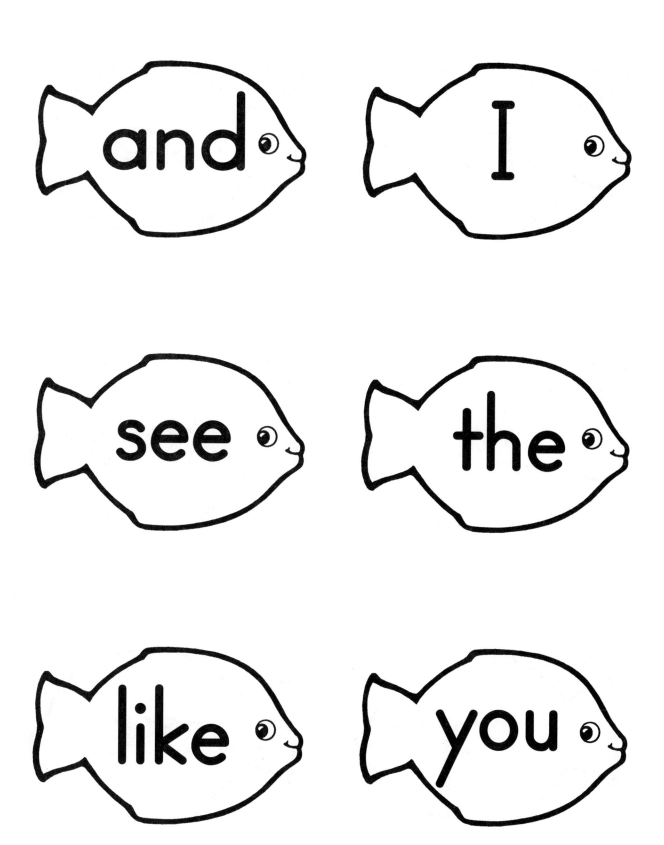

Sight Word Fish *(cont.)*

Phoneme Manipulation

Objective: Segmenting and spelling words

Rationale: The ability to use letters and sounds will increase as students segment words and match letters to sounds.

Materials: A set of alphabet cards for every student

Preparation: If you don't have multiple sets of lowercase letters, make duplicate sets of pages 29–31. (You may prefer to have partners share one set of alphabet cards the first time you try this activity.)

Procedure:

- Put the letters in alphabetical order on the floor, lowercase letters showing. You can have a few students do this for you before beginning with the first group, or you can extend the time for the first group so they can put the letters in alphabetical order.

- Seat each student in front of a set of letters.

- **Today we're going to spell words. Our first word is** *dog*. **What three sounds do you hear?** Wait for student response.

- **Look at the letters. Which one makes the first sound of dog? Find the *d* and put it in front of you.**

- **Let's say the three sounds for the word *dog* again. What sound comes after /d/?**

- **What letter makes the /o/ sound? Find the *o* and put it behind the *d*.**

- **What is the last sound you hear? What letter makes the /g/ sound? Put the *g* behind the *o*.**

- **Let's name the letters together. D...o...g. Let's sound this word out again. /D/ /o/ /g/, dog.**

- **Let's change the word *dog* to *fog*. What three sounds do you hear in fog? Do you hear a /d/ sound? Put the *d* back in its place in the alphabet since we don't need it.**

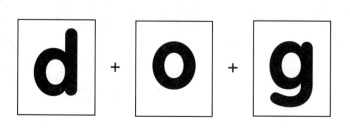 

Phoneme Manipulation *(cont.)*

- **What is the first sound you hear in** *fog*? **What letter makes the /f/ sound? Find the letter** *f*. **Put it at the beginning of your word.**

- **Let's sound** *fog* **out again. /F/ /o/ /g/. Let's spell the word** *fog*. **F…o…g. Do the three letters match the three sounds?**

- Continue by changing another letter. Each time, have students segment the word. After two or three changes, put all letters back in order and begin with a new word.

- Try the following words:

red	fan	hot
bed	man	pot
fed	ran	lot
pit	nut	ham
hit	hut	jam
sit	cut	Sam*

- After completing all the words listed, you can make more words by starting with any three-sound word and changing one letter at a time. You can change ending sounds and middle sounds, as long as the word makes sense.

- Each time have the students put the extra letters back in alphabetical order.

*If the letters have capital letters on one side and lowercase letters on the other side, make sure the capital side is showing for the first letter of a name.

Word Box Spelling

Objective: Spelling words with letters

Rationale: The ultimate purpose of phonemic awareness is to guide students to the reading of words, using letters. This activity will give students practice spelling common consonant, vowel, consonant words.

Materials: Word cards (pages 194–196), small magnetic letters, word boxes

Preparation: Copy the word cards and cut them apart. To make boxes, use small, metal, mint boxes. Cover the top of each box with solid contact paper. On the inside of each lid, Velcro or tape a word card. Inside the box, place the magnetic letters to spell the word.

Procedure:

- Seat the students around a table. **We are going to use word boxes to spell words. Each of these boxes contains a picture under the lid, and the letters inside to spell the word.**

- **I will open my box and show you how to play. I have the box with the picture of a cat under the lid. Cat. /C/.../a/.../t/. Now, I will take the letters out of the box and close the lid, placing the letters on the top.**

- **Now it is time to give myself a test. I must remember the word is (cat). I hear the sounds /C/.../a/.../t/. Now, I will spell it with the magnetic letters. I will put c...a...t in order on top of my lid.**

- **Okay, now I am ready to check my work. I will simply lift the lid to see the spelling for the word cat.**

- **Now it is your turn. Choose a box and try to spell the word inside.**

- Let each student choose a word box, and allow him or her to work independently. Give assistance as necessary. The students can trade boxes and spell words as long as time permits.

Note: The mint boxes make this a unique activity for the students. However, you can complete it without the boxes if necessary. Instead, have the students turn the card face down and spell the word on the table or floor with letters, then turn the card face up to check.

Word Cards

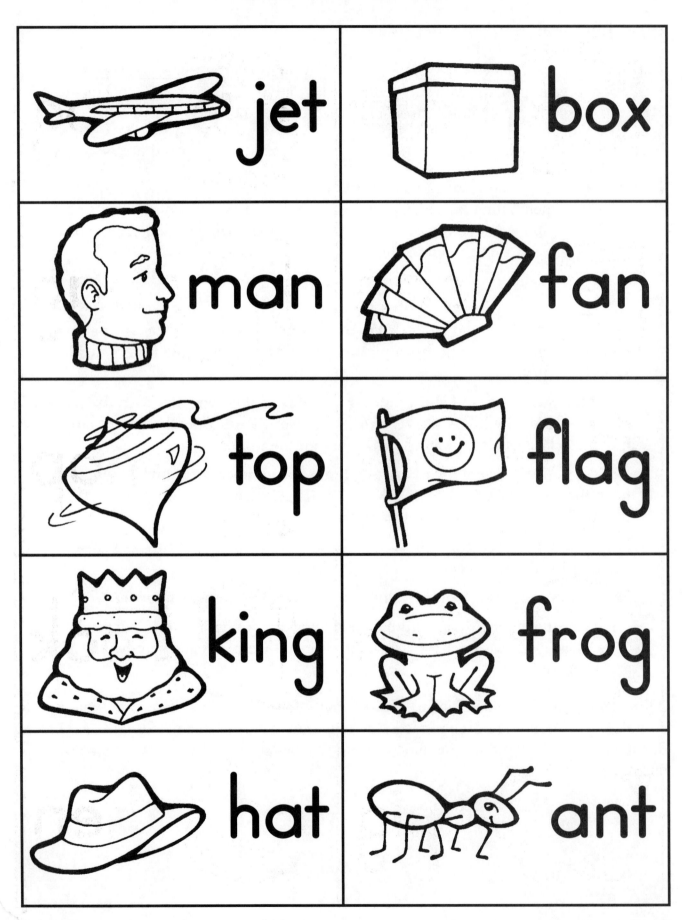

jet

box

man

fan

top

flag

king

frog

hat

ant

Word Cards *(cont.)*

cat

dog

can

bag

fox

mop

moon

book

pig

hen

Word Cards *(cont.)*

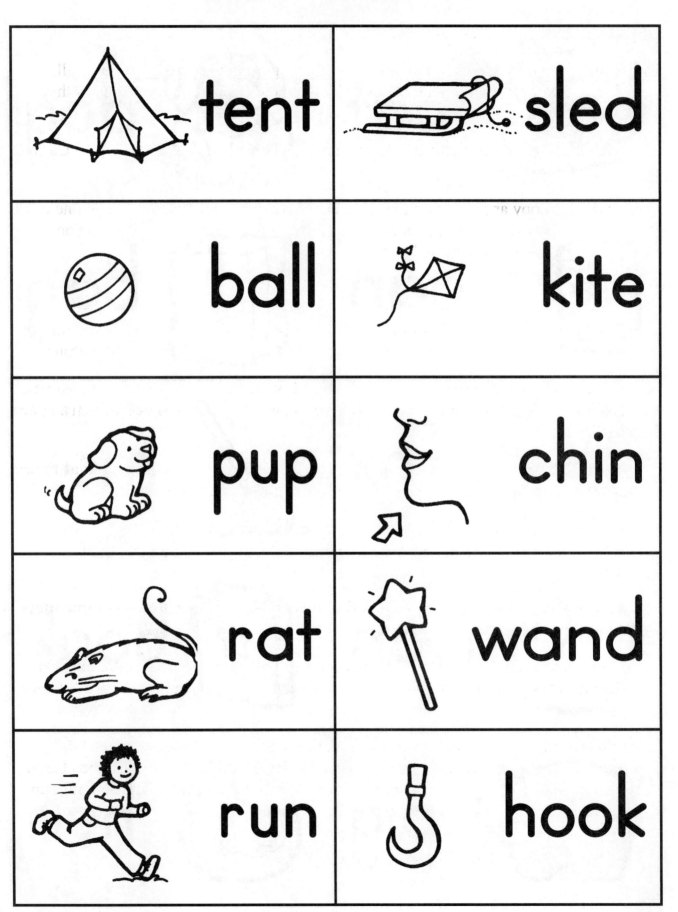

tent	sled
ball	kite
pup	chin
rat	wand
run	hook

Letter Blending Game

Objective: Blending letters to make words

Rationale: Blending letters to make words is an important beginning reading skill. Students will have an opportunity to practice sounding out words as they have fun playing a game.

Materials: Game pieces, number die, game board, Three and Four Sound Word Cards (pages 198–201)

Preparation: Copy and cut apart the word cards. Laminate, if desired. Make one copy of the blank game board (page 108) for each player, or substitute one large, blank game board.

Procedure:

- Seat the students at a table or on the floor. Give each student a game board (or put the single game board in the middle). Place the cards in the center of the group.

- **Today we're going to play a game. We will be blending letters to make words. Each time you figure out a word, you will move your game piece an extra space on the board.**

- **(Student's name), you will be first. Shake the number die and move that many spaces. Draw a card. Do you know the word? Can you sound it out?**

- If the student cannot identify the word, ask him/her to name each letter and/or its sound. Have the student blend the sounds together. Help with blending, if necessary.

- **You're right! The word is (repeat the word). Move your game piece one more space on the board.**

- Turn to the next child. **(Student's name), you will be next. Shake the number die and move that many spaces. Draw a card. Do you know the word? Can you sound it out?**

- Offer as much assistance as necessary, but have the student attempt to read the word. Once again, have the student name the letters and/or the sounds, then blend them together. Continue around the group. When the game is completed, mix up the cards and begin again if time permits.

Three and Four Sound Word Cards

cat	dog
pig	rat
wig	pen
log	mat

Three and Four Sound Word Cards *(cont.)*

sat	can
rag	got
yak	wet
pip	pop

Three and Four Sound Word Cards *(cont.)*

jig	tag
cog	men
gum	lag
hand	drop

flag	bib
bag	frog
let	man
hot	leg

Sound Box Spelling

Objective: Segmenting and spelling words

Rationale: The ability to use letters and sounds will increase as students segment words and write letters for sounds.

Materials: Sound Box Spelling work sheets (pages 203–204), a pencil for each student

Preparation: Make a copy of the Sound Box Spelling work sheets for every student.

Procedure:

- Seat the students around a table. Hand out the work sheet with the cat at the top. **Today we're going to spell words. Look at the cat at the top of the page. How many sound boxes do you see beside the cat? You're right, there are three. Let's make the three sounds for *cat*.**

- **Which letter makes the first sound of *cat*? Write the letter *c* in the first box.**

- **Let's say the three sounds for *cat* again. Which letter spells the middle sound? Write the letter *a* in the second box.**

- **What letter makes the last sound of *cat*? Write the letter *t* in the last box.**

- **Let's name the letters together. Let's sound this word out together.**

- **Let's try that again with the next picture. What three sounds do you hear in (name the next word)?**

- **What letter makes the first sound? Write it in the first box.**

- **Segment the word again with me. What letter makes the second sound? Write it in the second box.**

- **What letter makes the last sound? Write it in the last box.**

- **Let's name all the letters again. Let's sound this word out together.**

- Follow this same sequence for each picture.

Sound Box Spelling

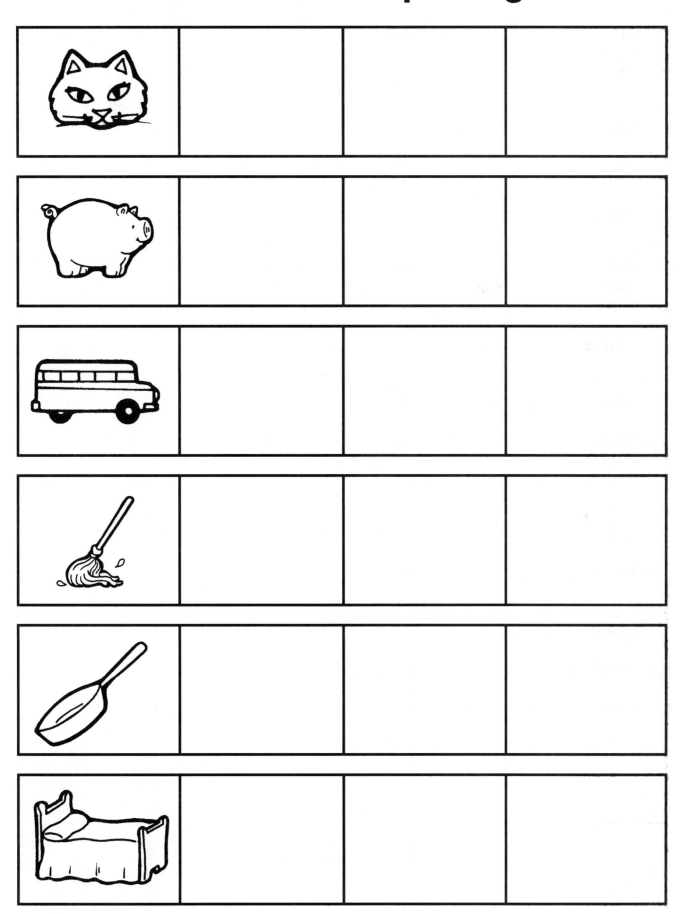

Sound Box Spelling *(cont.)*

Writing Words

Objective: Writing words

Rationale: The ultimate purpose of phonemic awareness is to guide students to the reading and writing of words, using letters. This activity will give students practice writing words they have learned in school during the year.

Materials: A pencil, a small, blank booklet for each child

Preparation: To make the booklets, make one copy of page 206 for each student. Put the cover with two pieces of paper; fold and staple to make a writing booklet.

Procedure:

- Seat the students around a table.

- **Today we are going to practice writing many of the words we know!**

- **We have worked hard this year, and we have learned to spell many words. Let's take a minute and talk about some of the words we can spell.**

- Give the students a chance to brainstorm many of the words they are able to write independently. If the students cannot think of words, direct them to the class word bank.

- **Wow! We have talked about a lot of words. Now it is time for you to record some of these words in a booklet.**

- Pass out the blank booklets to children and encourage them to begin writing. As the allotted time concludes, encourage the students to take their booklets home and have their parents help them write more words.

My
Book of
Words

Name

Index

Index (cont.)